W9-CBV-249

REFUGE
FROM ABUSE

Healing and Hope for Abused Christian Women

Nancy Nason-Clark &
Catherine Clark Kroeger

InterVarsity Press
Downers Grove, Illinois

InterVarsity Press
P.O. Box 1400, Downers Grove, IL 60515-1426
World Wide Web: www.ivpress.com
E-mail: mail@ivpress.com

©2004 *by Nancy Nason-Clark and Catherine Clark Kroeger*

*All rights reserved. No part of this book may be reproduced in any form without written permission from
InterVarsity Press.*

*InterVarsity Press® is the book-publishing division of InterVarsity Christian Fellowship/USA®, a student
movement active on campus at hundreds of universities, colleges and schools of nursing in the United States
of America, and a member movement of the International Fellowship of Evangelical Students. For information
about local and regional activities, write Public Relations Dept., InterVarsity Christian Fellowship/USA, 6400
Schroeder Rd., P.O. Box 7895, Madison, WI 53707-7895, or visit the IVCF website at <www.ivcf.org>.*

*Scripture quotations, unless otherwise noted, are from the New Revised Standard Version of the Bible,
copyright 1989 by the Division of Christian Education of the National Council of the Churches of Christ in
the USA. Used by permission. All rights reserved.*

Design: Cindy Kiple
Images: Enrique Ranzoni/Digital Vision

ISBN 0-8308-3203-3

Printed in the United States of America ∞

Library of Congress Cataloging-in-Publication Data
Nason-Clark, Nancy, 1956-
   Refuge from abuse: healing and hope for abused Christian women/
   Nancy Nason-Clark and Catherine Clark Kroeger.
      p. cm.
   Includes bibliographical references.
   ISBN 0-8308-3203-3 (pbk.: alk. paper)
   1. Abused wives—Religious life. 2. Christian women—Religious
   life. I. Kroeger, Catherine Clark. II. Title.
   BV4596.A2N37 2004
   261.8'327—dc21

                                                      2004006381

P 19 18 17 16 15 14 13 12 11 10 9 8 7 6 5 4 3 2 1

Y 19 18 17 16 15 14 13 12 11 10 09 08 07 06 05 04

OVERTON MEMORIAL LIBRARY
HERITAGE CHRISTIAN UNIVERSITY
P.O. Box HCU
Florence, Alabama 35630

CONTENTS

PATHWAY TO HOPE

ABUSE IS UGLY. IT IS ALWAYS WRONG. It is never part of God's design for healthy family living. It distorts relationships and shatters dreams. It creates pain and despair. It never produces hope. You know this all too well—that's why you've picked up this book.

Abuse leaves emotional scars that can last a lifetime. Fear is the most common response to violence in the family. Victims also experience shame, betrayal and a sense of hopelessness. Sometimes it is just so hard to know which way to turn, whom to trust. That's why we have written this book—to offer hope in the midst of crisis.

Abuse often travels from one generation to the next. Witnessing violence harms children, even if they're not the ones being struck or cursed. When abuse occurs in a family, everyone is harmed.

When abuse occurs in a Christian family, the woman victim may turn to the church or its leaders for help. There are so many questions: Why has God abandoned me? What did I do to deserve this? Must I continue to love until death do us part? What does God expect of me?

In the pages to follow, we offer some answers to these questions, some ideas to strengthen you to move on in your life and faith, some insights from the Scriptures. We believe the Bible's message is clear: God speaks out against violence. Peace and safety are the biblical building blocks for family living. When there is no peace or safety, a relationship is not healthy.

The journey toward hope, healing and wholeness will be long and hard. There are few simple answers. There will be many struggles. Your faith will be tested. Sometimes your church family will be of great help, but at times they may hinder your healing or offer advice that threatens

A relationship is not healthy when . . .

You are belittled, and your value and your accomplishments are not recognized.

You are threatened.

You are slapped, pushed, kicked or hurt.

You are kept away from your family and friends.

There is extreme possessiveness or jealousy.

Your partner insists on being together all the time, or on monitoring what you do when you are alone.

You, your family, your work, your church and your friends are disrespected.

You are ignored when you give an opinion; your likes and dislikes count for nothing.

You are called names that are embarrassing and hurtful.

You are blamed for all the problems.

your emotional or physical well-being. That's why we believe that you need resources and guidance to chart the journey from fear to safety. We like to call it the pathway to hope. On this path, victims are transformed into survivors. We invite you to begin the journey.

Writing this book has been an interesting journey for us too. We bring different backgrounds and experiences: Nancy is a sociologist, Cathie a biblical scholar. We are citizens of two different nations, trained in different fields, born in different generations, worshiping in different traditions. But we share a common conviction: Christian love should not hurt.

For most of our adult lives, we have been hearing real-life stories about abuse in the communities where we live and work, in the churches we visit, in the workshops we lead, over coffee at conferences and women's gatherings. Women have told us of their pain and brokenness but also of hope and help they have found in the midst of great trials.

We have also studied abuse more formally. For many years Nancy has been researching abuse in Canada, the United States and other cultures. With her research team, she has interviewed hundreds of women victims and hundreds of clergy. Through mailed questionnaires, focus groups, in-depth interviews, telephone surveys and community consultations, she has learned how abuse happens in households of faith. Meanwhile, Cathie has been doing biblical study on violence. Through her teaching and writing, she has been helping seminary students and church leaders interpret what the Bible really says about abuse. Bringing our experiences together, we are able to offer information and support to help you begin your journey of hope or to sustain you through times of disappointment and despair.

At the request of our editor, Jim Hoover, whom we both respect deeply and thank wholeheartedly for his guidance, we have kept notes and scholarly jargon to a bare minimum. We hope that you will find our book easy to read and that our desire to support you will be clear on every page. The concepts we discuss and the ideas for pressing forward that we offer have been developed through many years of carefully conducted scholarship. In the chapters to follow, there are numerous stories of real people, their lives and their struggles. Sometimes there are quotes from interviews or focus groups. Details of the stories have been changed slightly to protect the anonymity of the men and women involved.

We think the combination of sociological studies and biblical scholarship brings special insights for abuse victims on the road to recovery. As you read our book, it will become clear that it is written in two different voices—our voices, separate and distinct, but with shared purpose and vision. Both of us write in the first person.

Each chapter provides you with examples of women at various stages of the healing journey. At times you may wonder why we give so many examples. Our hope is that you will find one or more stories that speak directly to your experience.

We also offer insights for confronting the issues and deciding what to do. These are the basic things that you must know in order to move on to God's place of abundance. Many women feel lost because they do not know where to turn for help—or if it's even appropriate for a Christian woman to look for help.

Each chapter closes with a section for spiritual reflection. As you wrestle with grief, anger, fear, bitterness, bewilderment, guilt, shame, despair and disillusionment, you may feel a deep suspicion about the Bible and those who have interpreted it to you. We hope to give you a new perspective on the Bible so that it proves to be a resource for help and healing, a source of God's comfort, not of further abuse.

The biblical meditations invite you to look at the Scriptures with new eyes. The psalmist prayed, "Open my eyes, so that I may behold wondrous things out of your law" (Psalm 119:18). Sometimes it takes a new way of looking at things to see the help God has available. When hostile forces surrounded the house of Elisha, the prophet prayed that God would open the eyes of his panic-stricken servant. With his new God-given vision, the servant saw that "the mountain was full of horses and chariots of fire all around Elisha" (2 Kings 6:17). In the same way, the Lord opened Hagar's eyes to see a well that enabled her and her son to survive in the wilderness. Like Hagar, you may see resources that you did not realize were there for you. You may discover for yourself new truths in the Scriptures.

The apostle Paul tells us that the biblical accounts are not just instructive tales but are given to us as spiritual examples. "These things happened to them to serve as an example, and they were written down to instruct us, on whom the ends of the ages have come" (1 Corinthians 10:11). The ancient stories given by the Holy Spirit can still empower us. Like Rizpah, you can stand for what is right. Like Abigail, you can take prompt and decisive action when it's needed. Like Joseph, you can test the waters on the long voyage to forgiveness. You can reach out to Jesus like the woman who had been hemorrhaging for years. In the story of Leah you may find a paradigm for the healing of a troubled marriage. In the anguish and distress of David, you can find echoes of your own experience—and with the words of David's songs, your soul can soar to heaven. Take your time with these biblical reflections. Let God speak to your soul.

❦

Researching and writing a book involves debts to many people. I (Nancy) wish to thank those who have funded my research over the past decade[1] and in particular to acknowledge the financial support of the Louisville Institute for the Study of Protestantism and American Culture. Most of all, I am grateful to the men and women who have opened up their lives to my research team and shared from their hearts or from their professional experiences the reality of violence. Thank you for the honor of listening to your pain and to your hope.

Over the past decade the following people have been involved in the collection of data or its analysis: Lois Mitchell, Lori Beaman, Christy Hoyt, Amanda Steeves, Michelle Spencer-Arsenault and Lisa Hanson. They know how much I have appreciated their labors, their humor and their insights, but readers need to know that as well. In preparing this book, I have been grateful for the excellent research assistance of Barbara Fisher-Townsend and Lanette Ruff, and the supportive work environment of the Department of Sociology at the University of New Brunswick. On the home front, I owe special thanks to my husband, David, and our daughters, Natascha and Christina. There is also a supportive cast of friends and colleagues in various locations around the world, who over the years have become dearer.

I (Cathie) wish to thank the many persons, both female and male, who have shared their suffering with me. Each has something to teach me, and each drives me back to the question: How can we as Christians respond to such circumstances? What does this mean in light of our conviction that the Bible is our only infallible rule of faith and practice? This is the challenge to those who seek to walk by faith.

I must also thank those experienced in the field of domestic violence, for they gave me much-needed information. In particular, I would like to thank Independence House in Hyannis, Massachusetts, for all that the staff and volunteers have taught me. Their wisdom and dedication truly astound me—their willingness day and night to save human life and provide support in the most grueling situations. I am inspired by the work of my own sister, Elizabeth Clark Blank, who has given much of her life to the protection of abused women. I think with gratitude of all those heroic pioneers who dared to take up the cause while the church lagged far behind in its concern. May God forgive us and guide our actions and attitudes!

– One –

HOW DO I KNOW
I NEED HELP?

YOU MAY FEEL ALONE, ABANDONED AND AFRAID. Maybe you are blaming yourself for the abuse you have suffered. Maybe you feel overwhelmed by shame. You may feel pressured to keep silent about all that has happened to you. What energy you have is consumed by keeping up appearances, pretending that everything at home is all right. You may feel let down by your church and misunderstood by your closest friends. If only you could turn back the clock. If only you could make things better. If only you could protect the children. If only the violence would stop.

You are not alone. Millions of women around the world, many of them Christian, have been hit or bullied by a man who promised before God that he would love and cherish his wife until death parted them. Still, most battered wives feel alone. Since abuse occurs behind closed doors, others in the community or at church don't see it happening. So victims feel faceless and nameless. Silence and secrecy abound.

Christmas was just around the corner. A women's banquet had been organized at our church as an outreach to abuse victims. Some were staying in a battered women's shelter; others had moved on to "second stage housing," apartments available to them for up to eighteen months. Christmas is a good time of year to make connections between the church and the community. It is an especially difficult season for those experiencing family turmoil or loss of intimate relationships. For a woman who is enduring violence or suffering at home, Christmastime adds pressure and heartache.

As I drove to the church, thinking about the talk I'd be giving, my mind was filled with questions: *How can we church women strengthen our relationship with the shelter? What are some of the ways women of faith can offer support to abused women around us? How can my talk tonight be both a challenge to nonviolated women and a comfort to those who have been battered? And how can we all reduce family violence in our neighborhoods and congregations?*

Beside me in the front seat of the car was an Amish doll that I had brought as a prop for the talk. This faceless doll with a wide-brimmed bonnet has no facial features—no nose, no eyes, no smile. Her face is simply a piece of plain off-white cloth. The design is meant to represent one of the hallmarks of Amish culture: submission of the self to the preservation of the group.

Somehow the simplicity of the doll linked in my mind to the story of the birth of Jesus, the reason for the evening's celebration. Mary, a young Jewish girl of ordinary circumstances, was chosen to bear the Christ child. *I wonder how she felt. I wonder who she told. I wonder if she wept.* There is a lot to wonder about.

As I drove, I imagined one of my daughters being in Mary's situation: an angelic visit, a teenage pregnancy, a long trip away from home, no room in the inn. *Chosen indeed.* Then I thought about the parallels between Mary's extraordinary story and a battered woman's tale: the disbelief, the unknown, the fear, shame, isolation.

Suddenly I flashed back to a day in my life as a student, years earlier.

I walked into a cozy craft shop in Intercourse, Pennsylvania, a town in Amish country. In the center of the shop's basement was a large wooden frame supporting and stretching the top of a brightly colored quilt. Sitting around it were six Amish women, varying in age from about twenty to eighty. They were speaking German. Once they were aware of my presence, though, they fell silent; I was an intruder. Since I was making them uncomfortable, I cut short my admiration of their work.

On the sidewalks outside, young girls carried groceries in hand-woven baskets; older women held a bolt or two of fabric under their arms as they climbed into horse-drawn buggies; men tended the animals and gathered supplies for the farm. At first it was like a walk through a reconstructed historic village. But there is far more to the story of the Amish than such a quick glimpse can show. The people live by a series of principles and practices that reinforce submission of the self in the service and preservation of Amish culture. The blank stare of the doll and the silence of the adult women haunt me: so many stories hidden, tales not told, pains and joys not expressed.

Back in the present, sitting at a red light, I pondered how to communicate with strength and grace the notion of facelessness to the women at the banquet. One group of them—those who had experienced battery—would know from personal experience what the Amish doll represented. They too had been unable to look at themselves fully and completely, unable to gaze into the mirror of their life and record or remember precisely what they saw. In the case of Amish women, the mirror represents the forbidden. As a battered woman, you too may have avoided self-reflection because it evokes too much pain, too much despair. No doubt you understand all too well from your own experience the blankness of the gauze cloth covering the place where the doll's face ought to be.

The evening proceeded as planned. I set the Amish doll on the lectern. She illustrated Mary, the young woman chosen to bring to human life God's Son; she illustrated the anonymous battered woman whose call for help cannot be heard; she also represented the unnamed woman who reaches out her hand to help a sister in need.

❦

When a family is in crisis, does anyone know? What does the cry for help sound like? What does the despair of a battered woman look like? Is there any way to identify women who are living in fear? When some women face life-threatening danger, they ask for help. Others suffer in silence. Some knock on doors; others wait for rescue to come to them. What have you chosen to do?

> To find your voice
> is no small feat
> amidst the turmoil and the pain;
>
> To listen to the words you speak
> enables me to gain
> The credibility I require
> to silence your oppressors—
> especially those inside your head;
>
> So that once found
> you never lose
> your words or voice again.

Now there was a great wind, so strong that it was splitting mountains and breaking rocks in pieces . . . but the LORD was not in the wind; and after the wind an earthquake, but the LORD was not in the earthquake; and after the earthquake a fire, but the LORD was not in the fire; and after the fire a sound of sheer silence. (1 Kings 19:11-12)

❦

Opening our eyes to violence in the family setting is never easy. Usually it comes with a cost. For some women, that cost is personal: when they attempt to see the suffering of others, the faces of their own loved ones come into focus. In agony they relive their own childhood or adolescent vulnerabilities. Such intrusive, painful memories threaten to interrupt or control, once again, their daily lives and future possibilities. For these women, violence can only be thought of as *my* abuse, as if there were no other story than one's own.

Others find it very difficult to picture violence in the family setting because they have not suffered the clinging tentacles of its humiliation. They want to understand and empathize, but their hearts are cold—not because they are callous or indifferent by nature but because they have never heard the heart-cry of a victim, told in the first person, face to face, with tears and long silences. These disclosures are so different from the news reports that flow from the lips of a broadcaster, or the clipped scenes of a television documentary. If a person has never heard or seen a victim disclose, it is nearly impossible to comprehend the shame, or the fear, or the impact.

As a victim of abuse, you need to realize that it is very hard for someone else to understand the full impact of your pain or its long-term consequences.

THE STORIES OF TWO ABUSED WOMEN

Mildred Jennings[1] was a deeply spiritual person. She was described by her pastor as "a beautiful Christian, very active in the church." She had five grown children, all of them high achievers. But about three months after her minister had moved to the area, Mildred began to tell him some things about her marriage, and before long she revealed that things were not as they seemed.

She was regarded as a balanced person, but Russell, her husband, was a very controlling man. He hungered after power and status. To satisfy his desire for flashy goods, he was continually borrowing money, and as a result the family was going further and further into debt.

One day Mildred was talking on the phone with her eldest daughter, a physician in a neighboring region. Apparently, Mildred had gone to a hiding place in her home to retrieve some notes about past abusive incidents. Russell came home to find her on the telephone with the papers scattered on the desk in front of her. He flew into a rage—almost as severe as a time he had tried to kill her.

One Sunday morning Russell gave his sixty-year-old wife and her eighty-three-year-old live-in mother two hours to leave the family home forever. The pastor found a note on the pulpit asking him to meet with Mildred after the second service. They met, he listened to her story, and that afternoon he took the two frightened women to the home of a church family who were willing to host them for a few days. In the pastor's words, "I remember the very first day, when I was driving her . . . saying someday you'll see this was the best thing that ever happened to you. But it was a terrible time, terrible time."

The minister saw Russell's problem as his desire to control his wife. He controlled the money. He controlled where Mildred went and with whom. He tried to keep her from going to church, going to movies and going to visit her friends. When Mildred resisted his control, he would become very loud and threatening, or he would turn silent and refuse to talk to her, sometimes for up to a month.

As a result, Mildred felt she was worthless. In the pastor's words, "Her self-esteem was [already] low because she had grown up in a family where there was abuse. . . . She had seen her grandfather knock her grandmother out, leave her on the floor in a pool of blood. She saw her father treat her mother very negatively . . . so she had very low self-esteem." Russell, too, was a childhood victim of abuse; as a little boy he had learned to use his fists to get what he wanted.

After Mildred and her mother had been kicked out of their home, she spent the next four or five months feeling sorry for her husband. The pastor recalled, "Even though he was the one that put her [out] with two hours' notice, she felt that she was hurting him by having blabbed. . . . I felt so bad for her, she was so vulnerable. And he was always calling her . . . she would pity him so much. Pity him because he never knew what love was as he was growing up."

Mildred had turned to the minister for help because she knew nowhere else to turn. At her point of deepest need, she looked to the church and found that her pastor was willing to help her begin the long journey toward healing and wholeness. Mildred had many questions: Could God forgive her for leaving Russell? What about her marriage vows, especially the part that says for better, for worse, for the rest of your life? Why was God letting this happen?

What did her pastor's care do for Mildred? "I did a lot of listening," the pastor confided. "I reminded her that she would have never have left

Safety must be the first priority

HERE ARE SOME QUESTIONS YOU SHOULD ASK YOURSELF ABOUT SAFETY . . .

Is it safe these days for you to be home or to return home? Are your children safe at home?

Has your husband's anger ever frightened you or made you feel unsafe? Do you think maybe your husband could harm himself or damage your property?

Do you have a safety plan in case you need to leave home quickly? Do you have access to a car at all times? Is there public transportation close to where you live, or a taxi service?

Do you know how to contact the transition house in your community or another nearby community, in case you need shelter?

that day. . . . It wasn't her . . . decision." Through counseling, the minister
tried to challenge Mildred's incorrect beliefs—that she was at fault, responsible for her husband's misery, or that the breakup was her doing.

For the first few months the minister and Mildred talked every day.
After that for over two years there was contact at least once a week,
sometimes for fifteen or twenty minutes, sometimes for over an hour.
Russell, meanwhile, blamed the abuse and its heartache on Mildred, on
other people, on everyone but himself. He was unwilling for the minister
or anyone else to offer him assistance. He preferred to be left alone.

Mildred received care and counseling from her pastor for quite a long
time. The minister also talked with other professionals so that they could
understand Mildred's situation better. Her lawyer, for example, couldn't
understand her Christian values, especially how she could so easily forgive this abusive man. With Mildred's permission, the minister explained
her values to the lawyer, even as he tried to challenge them through
counseling. He actually encouraged Mildred to be *less* forgiving, helping
her see that God was not asking her to ignore the pain and the abusive
events but to hold her husband accountable for his behavior.

For Mildred and her mother, rescue was the first need, but on the
road to healing and recovery, spiritual needs were primary. Mildred's
mistaken religious beliefs could have kept her from growing into wholeness. Faulty religious thinking can be best challenged by a pastor or
someone else with spiritual credentials. As for many Christian women
who are abused, *the language of the spirit,* God's word of help and encouragement, was what Mildred needed to supplement *the language of contemporary culture.*

❦

Brenda Steppe,[2] in her early twenties, a recent graduate with an accounting degree, was in the fifth month of her first pregnancy. She was living
with a man, Carson, who was younger than she in both age and maturity.
When Ruth, the pastor of the local church, first saw Brenda, she was

standing alone on the side of the street, one shoe missing, deeply distraught. "There was a pregnant lady standing on the side of the street in the rain, bawling her eyes out. And the reason she was bawling her eyes out was because her common-law partner had just come home drunk and bonked her down on the floor and proceeded to kick her in the stomach. Okay. That's how I got involved. That's how I intervened. I chose them. They didn't choose me."

This is a story of two women who enter each other's life and are never quite the same. Brenda was discovered with a multitude of emotional and physical problems and dilemmas—by all counts she was needy. Ruth was motivated by compassion, fueled by spiritual zeal, to make the world a better place.

Ways to protect yourself . . .

Find the phone number for the local shelter. When you are able, call them and ask about their services. Then if you ever need their help, you will already know what services they offer.

Remember that you can call 911 any time you are in danger. Also you can call the shelter and get information from a worker even if you are not planning to seek refuge there.

It was the Christmas season, cold and snowy. The pastor had been walking in the downtown area of a small city when her eyes fell upon Brenda. She approached and cautiously asked what was wrong. At first Brenda did not want to speak with this stranger, not knowing that she was a pastor and could help. But Ruth persisted, having noticed the bruises and then the pregnancy.

Brenda's abusive boyfriend had driven her out of the house without any warning. She had lost one of her shoes running out the door as he threw a beer bottle at her. The pastor recounted how Brenda wanted her to buy a pair of sunglasses before she got on the bus. Brenda's first reaction was to hide the shame, to block her pain from view and cover over her feelings of failure.

Once the glasses had been purchased, the pastor accompanied her on the bus. When they arrived at the place Brenda called home, she wanted to clean up the mess Carlson had made when he hurled his supper at her. Fragments of food and china were strewn everywhere.

Why would a battered woman return to clean up such a mess? From Brenda's perspective, Carlson didn't know how to take care of the house, and furthermore, he was unable to complete the final preparations for Christmas, such as wrapping and delivering presents on time. "She would have moved right back into that hellhole," Ruth said later, "with herself about ready to have a baby." It was difficult—almost impossible—for Brenda to leave the abusive relationship because she felt as if *she* was abandoning *him*.

MILDRED, BRENDA AND MYTHS ABOUT ABUSE

Two women, Mildred and Brenda, who have experienced intimacy laced with violence. One is old; one is young. One has lived in comfortable surroundings, the other knows poverty. One has a dependent mother, the other is pregnant. Both are frightened. Both fear the future. One speaks, the other is trying to find her voice.

Their true stories help us to dispel some of the myths surrounding abuse—when it occurs, to whom it happens, how it can be stopped. From their stories we learn that abuse can happen to anyone.

Myths to be dispelled:

- Abuse doesn't happen in our region.
- Abuse doesn't happen in my neighborhood.
- Abuse doesn't happen in my church.
- Abuse could never happen in my family.
- Abuse could never happen to me.

Truths revealed:

- Abuse has no geographical boundaries.

- Abuse occurs in all social classes.

- Abuse occurs in all religious groups.

- Violence can happen in any family.

- Violence can happen to me.

Around the world, and in our own backyards, countless women are suffering the long-term consequences of violence in the family. Most often the abuse is caused by someone who is, or has been, loved and trusted. We can be very deeply hurt by those we love. Sometimes the wounds are inflicted by words that break our hearts; sometimes the wounds are inflicted by fists that break our bones.

Those of us who have never experienced violence in our home find it hard to believe that abuse is so common. Even those of us who are victims can find it hard to believe, for we feel isolated and alone. But the truth is that about one in four women worldwide has been the victim of some form of sexual or physical abuse. Countless more have suffered emotional or psychological abuse. Teenage women who are raped on a date, young pregnant women who are hit across the face by their husband, middle-aged mothers who live in fear, elderly widows who have their

Ask yourself some hard questions . . .

Do you live in fear?

Do you feel like you are walking on eggshells?

Are you afraid about what your children are hearing and seeing at home?

Has violence been getting more intense and more frequent?

Do you fear harm to your property or pets?

Is it time to get help?

assets stolen—violence takes many ugly forms in our communities, and sadly, in our churches too.

Churches claim that their mission is to heal the brokenhearted in the name of the gospel. Women and men of faith share this calling. The healing touch is extended in acts of compassion by ordinary people. Perhaps you can think of several examples of such compassion in your own life. As we extend God's healing touch, the world is changed, one family at a time.

Christians say that the family is very important to them. They even talk about "the church family," extending the warmth and nurturing of the home environment into the life of the congregation. This means church people have a special opportunity to put their energies into making every family safe. But it also means that when violence touches families of faith, victimized women and children can feel especially isolated from other believers.

Some women ask for help; others suffer in silence. Recognizing one's need for help is usually the first step in the healing process.

FOR SPIRITUAL REFLECTION

An abused woman tottered unsteadily under a blazing sun. An oasis rose in the distance, promising shade and water. Struggling with exhaustion, weak from her injuries, she navigated with shaky steps and at last sank down beside the well.

She had no idea what her next step might be, her strategy for survival. She only knew that she had made it to the well. Any planning beyond that would require more energy than she had. Friendless, homeless, pregnant, beaten, an unknown foreigner, she had few options. And she didn't have the emotional strength to be objective about her situation. One can't survive long without food and shelter—or without a sense of one's own worth.

Of all the persons introduced thus far in the book of Genesis, she is the most insignificant. We don't know anything of her family or spiritual background. Probably she was one of the slaves traded by Pharaoh in return for Sarah, Abraham's beautiful wife. When the patriarch allowed his wife to be received into Pharaoh's household, he was given sheep, oxen, donkeys, servants and camels. The property list places the slaves in between the male and female donkeys (Genesis 12:16). Hagar was thought no more significant than the animals.

This was how she had come into Abraham's household, and when Sarah was returned to her husband, Hagar remained as their slave. Pharaoh commanded Abraham to take his wife and leave Egypt, and so Hagar was transported to a strange country that bore no resemblance to her homeland.

But still Abraham and Sarah did not have what they wanted most—a son. Finally Sarah despaired of ever bearing a child and turned to what she considered the next best arrangement. In ancient Near Eastern law, a woman could give her husband her slave girl as a concubine, and if the slave conceived, when the child was born it was considered to belong to the mistress. So Hagar was used as sexual property, as a breeder for a desperate couple. Abraham was reluctant at first, but finally he gave in to his wife's insistence.

Hagar became pregnant, and she was pleased. Though she had been abused and exploited, at least she was capable of bearing a child when Sarah couldn't! Sarah noticed her complacency. The slave who had been nobody was now somebody, the mother of the master's child. Sarah keenly resented the slave's newfound assurance, her pride and joy in anticipating motherhood.

With Abraham's consent, Sarah found ways to turn the slave woman's life into a living hell. When Hagar could no longer endure the misery, she decided to run away. Desperation drove her into the desert, and she started along the way back to Egypt.

This was surely understandable, but it was terribly risky. There was no shelter for abused women, no place where she might go for refuge, no way to get food or water, no one to care for her during labor and delivery.

Before this, Bible history has been concerned with chieftains, heads of clans, patriarchs. And now into the center of the stage comes a nobody, a homeless African single mother who has been abused and exploited.

Hagar's first step had been to recognize that she was abused and needed to escape. At last she had found a well beside the road and collapsed, tired, thirsty, pregnant and scared.

Suddenly a voice called out, "Hagar, slave-girl of Sarah, where have you come from, where are you going?" Someone knew her name and was expressing concern. She was a real person to the stranger, whom she soon recognized as a messenger from God.

Unlike many others, Hagar was able to answer God honestly: "I am running away from my mistress, Sarah."

"Return to her," said the Lord. It sounded cruel, but in Sarah and Abraham's household she would be cared and provided for.

Like many another abused woman, Hagar found no option other than return. Although in the end she would gain her freedom as the proud mother of a free son, there were practical considerations first: food, shelter, care during the delivery and infancy of her son. God counseled her to return for the present, but she went back equipped with wonderful new resources.

First, she had a promise not only of a son but of grandchildren and great-grandchildren. Just as Abraham had been promised descendants so numerous that they could not be counted, so too Hagar was to become the ancestor of a great nation (Genesis 16:10). If Abraham was to become a patriarch, she was to become a matriarch in her own right, with honor and dignity. Hers was a special covenant with God. God promised, "I will so increase your descendants that they will be too numerous to count." It was the very same promise that had been made to Abraham. She too was to be founder of a mighty people.

Then came the prophecy of her son's freedom:

> *Now you have conceived and shall bear a son;*
> *you shall call him Ishmael,*

> *for the Lord has given heed to your affliction.*
> *He shall be a wild ass of a man. (Genesis 16:11-12)*

"Wild ass of a man"—what does that mean? It means that he would be free. In Job we read that no one can tame the wild ass nor bring it under the yoke into servitude (39:5-12).

Just as God knew the mother's name, so too a name was given to her son. The boy was to be called Ishmael—"God shall hear"—because God had heard Hagar's misery, both in Sarah's tent and there beside the well. She learned that God hears the cries of abused women.

Hagar dared to enter into a more intimate communion with God than most of the other Bible characters. "Have I really seen God?" she asked. And she did something none of the other people in the Bible had done: she gave God a name. "You are El-roi," she said, "the God who sees me." From that day on, the well was called Beer-lahai-roi, the Well of the One Who Sees Me. Hagar never forgot that she walked in God's sight.

She returned to her mistress, buoyed by the knowledge that God had both seen and heard her, and Abraham did name her baby Ishmael, "God shall hear." In her heart Hagar treasured the Lord's promise through all the difficult days of servitude and unkind treatment that followed.

In time Sarah herself conceived and bore a child, and at last she insisted that Ishmael and Hagar be evicted from the home. In point of fact, all of Abraham's sons by concubines were compelled to leave (Genesis 25:5-6). By sending Hagar away, Abraham was both freeing her and divorcing her. But God would use even this eviction for Hagar's healing.

If she and her son walked out of the camp as free human beings, that wasn't very comforting at the moment. The rope on the water skin dug into Hagar's shoulder. She had some water and a little bread, but before her stretched an enormous desert. The weight of the water slowed her down, as did the child who stumbled beside her. The water that she used to quench his thirst did not last long in the searing heat.

At last it was no use: the lad could go no further. Laying him under the shade of a scraggly bush, she sat down to mourn the impending death of the precious child God had given her. All the promises of God were coming true for Isaac, while her life and that of her son were about to be lost because of Sarah's spite. They would die like animals, as non-persons, with no meaning or dignity.

Hagar was a victim if ever there was one. She wept, and Ishmael wept. And God heard and called out, "What is the matter, Hagar? Don't be afraid. Lift up the boy and take him by the hand."

She was divorced, homeless, desperate, exhausted—and God was telling her to stand on her own two feet and lift up her son, "for I will make of him a great nation." The promise again, but how could it possibly be fulfilled?

Then God "opened her eyes," and she saw a well that she had failed to notice before. She now had access to a life-giving resource. It became for her a well of enablement. There they were able to establish a new life before God, for "God was with the boy."

Ishmael grew up and became a hunter. Hagar found herself a new person, able to direct her son's growth and to make important decisions. She chose a wife for him, according to cultural custom, and in time there was a great family.

We are told that whenever something happens for the first time in the Bible, it has great symbolic meaning. When God enabled her to use her own eyes, Hagar found the water, and it proved her salvation. In the desert environment of Bible times, water was not taken for granted. Again and again in the Bible, water is a symbol of spiritual life and of refreshment for the soul. God's people were invited to come to the waters (Isaiah 55:1). We read of joyfully drawing water from the wells of salvation (Isaiah 12:3), of finding rivers of water in the desert.

For waters shall break forth in the wilderness,
    and streams in the desert;
the burning sand shall become a pool,
    and the thirsty ground springs of water;

the haunt of jackals shall become a swamp,
　the grass shall become reeds and rushes. *(Isaiah 35:6-7)*

I will open rivers on the bare heights,
　and fountains in the midst of the valleys;
I will make the wilderness a pool of water,
　and the dry land springs of water. *(Isaiah 41:18)*

God has promised to lead us beside springs of water (Isaiah 49:10) and to grant abundance to each believer. Each will be like a hiding place from the wind, a shelter from the tempest, like streams of water in a dry place, like the shade of a great rock in a weary land (Isaiah 32:2).

Hagar became that shelter from the tempest, able to shelter both herself and her child, able to think clearly and act decisively. She had found the springs of living water.

HOW MUCH OF MY STORY
SHOULD I TELL?

ONCE YOU FINALLY GET UP THE COURAGE TO TELL A FRIEND, a family member or a pastor of your experiences of battery, you may be ridiculed, ignored or accused of lying. Could a man who seems so nice at church or at work actually be violent at home? The answer—though few are willing to say it—is yes. Yet in these days an increasing number of people are willing to listen, to believe and to help women who have been abused.

In this chapter you will meet three women, Claire, Carolyn and Martha, each at a point in her life where the abuse in her family is being revealed. As you will see, Claire tells part of her story, dropping hints that life is difficult and she is afraid of her husband's anger. Carolyn's story is told when the police are called by a third party; she doesn't want to talk about what is happening and resents the interference. Martha, on the other hand, takes immediate steps to seek help after a violent outburst, and she is forthright in explaining exactly what happened and why it must never happen again.

When is it safe to let someone know that you are frightened? Whom should you tell? What kind of response can you expect? Will there be enough resources to help you? What can—and do—churches and their leaders offer to victimized women and their families when violence in the family is revealed?

Every relationship contains paradoxes and contradictions, but within violent families these are especially powerful: "the love and sometimes the hate, the affection and sometimes violence, the pleasure and the wounding, the attachment that, in many cases, continues in spite of the abuse."[1]

As you read the stories of Claire, Carolyn and Martha, you may identify with the circumstances in one of their lives. Perhaps, like Claire, you have been dropping hints about the abuse and your fear, but no pastor or other church leader has picked up on your subtle cues. Perhaps, like Carolyn, a friend or neighbor has identified your need of help and maybe even given you this book. But at this point you do not want anyone to get involved. You already resent how much others know about your personal circumstances. Or maybe you are most like Martha. You know the violence is wrong, and you are determined to do something about it. Perhaps you have purchased this book as your first step in understanding what has happened in your marriage.

TELLING ONLY PART OF THE STORY

Claire and George Brown[2] were both schoolteachers. He had a history of alcohol abuse, and when he was drinking, he acted mean and nasty toward his family and often became violent. Claire went to talk to their pastor because she was concerned about how George's drinking was affecting Tommy and Mike, the couple's school-aged children. Were they frightened of their father? Would he ever deliberately harm them? Would her boys' childhood memories be haunted by the picture of their father in a drunken stupor?

As Claire recounted the story to her pastor, she emphasized the cycle that was controlling her life. George would always promise to change his ways, to stop his drinking. She never referred to herself as a battered woman: rather, she understood herself simply as the wife of a man with a drinking problem. But after her husband's alcohol abuse had been named and her fears identified and validated, she was able to talk about the abuse. She kept going back to the fear, the verbal assaults, the violence, the broken promises. Several times she and the boys had been very afraid.

For years, Claire and George had been on the fringes of church life: she came occasionally, sometimes with the boys, sometimes alone. But after one drinking-then-remorse-and-repentance episode, George began to join Claire in church attendance. Now Rev. Stephen Townie, the minister, became more involved with the Brown family. Pastor Steve began to drop in to the Brown home frequently when he did pastoral calls.

One evening he found George in a bad state. Rather than acting his usual "quiet drunk at home," the man was violent, and Claire and the children were full of fear.

Having witnessed the level of danger in the household, Steve encouraged Claire and the boys to leave with him and take refuge with his family at the parsonage. As Steve recounted this story later, he muses on his role as a protective shield for Claire, Tommy and Mike. The parsonage served as a temporary safe house, a place of security, if only for a short time.

Besides being an alcoholic, George spent money recklessly and had a gambling habit. If his behavior at home became public knowledge, he risked losing his teaching job. Claire believed that she deserved the abuse; this belief was part of the baggage she brought from growing up with an alcoholic father. Steve was surprised that a woman with a college degree would feel such personal responsibility for her husband's violence. But as he learned the details of her upbringing, he came to interpret Claire's self-blame as history repeating itself.

Home visitation was the avenue through which the pastor offered Claire safety. Paradoxically, the abusive home became a safe place to disclose abuse to a spiritual leader who was acting as a protective shield. Through his regular visits, Pastor Steve was able to pick up the clues

Claire offered and the unintended cues emanating from George.

Although Steve had encouraged Claire and the boys to leave the unsafe home permanently, she was unwilling to do that. So the pastor increased his home visits, each time assessing the level of risk, waiting for the right moment to speak and for when Claire would be ready for a referral.

Claire's story illustrates several realities:

- Woman abuse happens in middle-class families too.
- Many adult victims of abuse bear scars of dysfunctional childhood homes.
- Children are victims too, even when the abusive behavior isn't directed at them.
- The first time the victim asks for help, she may not name the abuse directly.
- The person who picks up on indirect clues may be ready and willing to help.

Claire's story may remind you of your own. Maybe you are married to a man who abuses alcohol. Maybe you have never thought of yourself as a battered woman, although your partner has shoved, hit or threatened you several times. Maybe you are worried about the children. With all these concerns on your heart, perhaps it is time that you disclose part of your story to someone else.

As you think this through, there are many things you will need to consider. Should you tell a friend first, or maybe your sister or cousin? Is your church a safe place to seek help? What resources are available in your area? Claire told her story in pieces, by dropping clues to her minister. The pastor was both perceptive and swift to act on the information she made available to him.

SOMEONE ELSE TELLING YOUR STORY

John and Carolyn Kent[3] had been married for just one week when the police were called to intervene in a violent outburst. In rural communities, it is not uncommon for people to know a lot about each other's lives. The officer in charge knew that Carolyn and John were parishioners of Seaside United Methodist Church and that their pastor was involved in the low-income housing project where they lived, so he chose to call their pastor for help. "I was there in two capacities," Rev. Smythe explained later. "I was there as a liaison from the housing authority board, and I was there as their minister."

The Kents had lived together before they were married and already had two young children, but they came to the church for their wedding. Both John and Carolyn were alcohol abusers, and each had had alcoholic parents. There was also a long history of sexual abuse on John's side and recently uncovered sexual abuse in Carolyn's family. At the time of the incident, John's mother was living with a physically abusive man. So violence was prevalent in both families.

According to the pastor, this couple seemed to lack even the most basic parenting skills. When he visited them, it wasn't unusual to see a baby bottle amidst all kinds of beer and other liquor bottles on the kitchen table.

When they were unemployed, which happened intermittently throughout the year, the drinking and the violence increased. Both suffered from low self-esteem, and both lacked positive role models.

In response to the call, the police and the minister got to the couple's home quickly. "By the time [I arrived] every window in the house had been smashed out. . . . He pinned her against the wall, but she had her fights too. . . . Both of them were bleeding," reported the pastor.

Carolyn had attacked John with a knife, and John had attacked both Carolyn and their house. There was extensive damage to the property. The children had not been harmed physically, but Rev. Smythe noted that John and Carolyn were "little volcanoes ready to explode." Without quick intervention, someone could have been killed.

Carolyn was not pleased to have the minister involved, but John's strong family background in the church paved the way for ongoing pastoral intervention and support. The minister was able to get John involved in a program that would help him recognize his abusive ways and avoid violence in the future. This program for men who battered (in another community) became his court-mandated treatment. Rev. Smythe was able to stay in touch, to monitor John's progress and offer supportive counsel.

Carolyn's story shows us several things:

- Violence in poor families is sometimes detected by an outside source as a result of the family's dependence on financial assistance provided by the state.

- Substance abuse and violence often coexist in families.

- Violence often travels from one generation to the next.

- Police are being trained to work with other professionals in order to respond to abuse.

- In rural communities, it's hard to keep abuse a secret.

- Pastors and priests often work with perpetrators of violence, not just abuse victims.

Homes can become extremely violent. It is much better for everyone if family members seek outside help before things escalate to the point where an outsider has to call the police.

Like Carolyn, you may have found others trying to rescue you or your children. Like Carolyn, you may have an anger problem yourself. You may be living in subsidized housing. And you may not be ready for a pastor to get involved.

But it's important to tell someone you trust about the violence and your fear. Don't delay any longer. There are many people willing and able to help you live free of abuse. Seek help soon. Find someone to talk to, someone you can trust.

TELLING THE WHOLE STORY

Martha and Mitchell Brook[4] were an elderly couple with no history of alcohol or drug abuse. Their relationship had had ups and downs over

Silent no longer

CHOOSING TO BREAK THE SILENCE INVOLVES . . .

reflecting on how much pain you have suffered

remembering the broken promises of your partner

considering the level of fear you feel

gathering your courage to take action

realizing that your children are being affected by the violence too

knowing there is hope for a life free of abuse

the years, but never any violence until Mitchell retired from his career as a high school guidance counselor. The trouble stemmed mostly from the fact that his whole sense of self-worth had been connected directly to his work. Once the work was taken away, he could not find anything that would give him that sense of worth or fill the void. It seemed as if all his hard work, his enthusiasm and his long hours on the job had vanished like a vapor. Tomorrow offered few promises, each day became a burden, each day offered only more time to spend with his wife.

While Martha had a number of women friends whom she met for lunch or shopping outings, Mitchell was isolated. He felt as if he were losing control over every aspect of his life. The dress shirts hung pressed in the closet, but there was nowhere to wear them. There wasn't any need to set the alarm clock to make sure the morning routine of shaving, showering and eating was completed by 7:15 a.m. Who would know, or care, if he slept until lunch?

Martha was a rather stern, no-nonsense woman; she had been employed as a nurse, but she too was now retired. For Martha, though, retirement brought time for the leisure activities and hobbies that she had been waiting for. Now she pursued them with a passion, alone or with friends. Since the children were grown and had families of their own in other parts of the country, the Brookses' nest was empty.

One day she called and made an appointment for both her and Mitchell to see their minister. Once inside the pastoral study, Martha told her minister about the incident that had prompted her call. She was a very strong woman and was able to say right out loud, "Well, you hit me!"

Mitchell was devastated at his wife's disclosure to the minister and humiliated by his own violent act. He knew Martha had no financial worries, since she had her own pension and would be able to support herself. Mitchell realized that he had a lot to lose if she left him. He knew that he was completely out of control and that if he did not change quickly, his wife *would* leave.

The pastor judged that the Brookses' relationship could be repaired. He thought what Mitchell most needed was an infusion of self-worth. So he suggested that Mitchell begin volunteering in the local elementary school, where there was a program for older men and women to read to the children and then listen to the children read aloud. He also introduced Mitchell to a group of retired men who had formed a breakfast club in a nearby church. These activities could draw on his skills as an educator and build up his self-esteem through friendship.

The pastor kept in touch with the Brookses and helped them with other relational struggles, and never again was there a violent act.

We learn several things from Martha's story:

- Loss of work or loss of self-esteem is sometimes related to violence.

- Abuse can happen at any age.

- Women who have their own income and savings are less likely to remain silent about their abuse.

- Sometimes abuse happens just once.

- Ongoing care from a pastor can be a very reassuring response to a woman who has been victimized.

As you read Martha's story and reflect on your own, you may be struck with how easily she was able to seek help. Her self-esteem was strong, she had an identity independent of Mitchell, and having had a good job for many years, she had financial resources that would enable her to care for herself.

Not all women can do what Martha did. But remember that it is *always* difficult to talk about problems in the family. Almost always our knee-jerk reaction is to hide our shame and maintain secrecy. Partly because Martha was willing to take immediate action, Mitchell's single act of violence was never repeated.

Disclosing Abuse

Telling someone of your abuse is very difficult to do. Many women keep the secret tightly guarded their whole lives.

In 1993 Statistics Canada conducted the first national survey of women's experiences of violence to be held anywhere in the world.[5] Through telephone interviews they obtained information from 12,300 women aged eighteen and up. According to their results, three in ten Canadian women currently or previously married or cohabitating have suffered at least one incident of physical or sexual violence at the hands of their partner. One in six currently married women disclosed abuse by her spouse, and one in two previously married women reported abuse in that relationship. One in three women victimized by their husbands feared for her own life at some point.

Women who reported having a violent father-in-law were at three times greater risk of abuse than women with a nonviolent father-in-law. Children witnessed the abuse of their mother in almost half of violent households. Women who lived with men who drank alcohol regularly were at greater risk than those living with men who did not drink at all. Almost one in two wife assault incidents resulted in injury, though in only one in four cases did these women seek medical attention.

Where did these women seek help? Some reported the violence to

Around the world women are abused

YOU ARE NOT ALONE . . .

Domestic violence is a leading cause of injury and death to women worldwide.[6]

The World Health Organization says that one in five women around the globe is physically or sexually abused in her lifetime.

Gender violence causes more death and disability among women aged 15-44 than cancer, malaria, traffic accidents or war.[7]

Women worldwide tell governments that family violence is one of their biggest concerns.[8]

Young wives (under 25) in Canada are at the greatest risk of murder by a violent husband.[9]

The U.S. surgeon general reports that domestic violence is the greatest single cause of injury among U.S. women, accounting for more emergency room visits than traffic accidents, muggings and rape combined.[10]

Female victims of homicide in the United States were significantly more likely to be killed by a husband, ex-husband or boyfriend than male victims were to be killed by their wife, ex-wife or girlfriend. In 2000, approximately 33 percent of female victims of homicide (1,247 women) were known to have been killed by a male intimate.[11]

the police, some to a community resource agency, a few told their physician or contacted a transition house. Hardly any women told their pastor. Amazingly, one in five victims had never disclosed their violence to anyone prior to disclosing it to an anonymous Statistics Canada telephone interviewer!

In the United States, one of the major researchers of family violence is Dr. Murray Straus of the Family Research Laboratory at the University of New Hampshire. His team has concluded that about one in six couples reports at least one violent incident per year, and one in four couples has at least one violent episode sometime during the relationship.[12] Scores of children see their father lash out at their mother or are the victims of parental rage themselves.[13] No faith community or neighborhood

Things to ponder if you are a victim of abuse . . .

Many women who have been violated by abusive acts do not feel that the term "abused woman" applies to them.

Looking for help soon after the first violent incident sends a clear message to the abuser and brings immediate support to you.

Children are victims too, even if they have never been hurt physically by the violent parent.

Be aware that responding to your needs as an abused woman can put others in danger of your husband's anger. Do not tell him where you have gone for help.

Don't look to only one person to meet all your needs. After you have told one person, try to figure out all the places where you might get help and all the people who can give you support.

is free of abuse. And while family violence most often occurs behind closed doors, the patterns are similar in bedrooms across the nation. Shame and secrecy are the immediate responses to the hurt and humiliation of victims. Many women spend so much energy trying to keep their abuse secret that they have no strength left to look for help. The problem is so widespread that some claim that all women live with either the fear or the reality of violence.[14]

Abuse is serious. It can be life threatening. And it can harm the lives of your children for a very long time.

Finding a safe place to tell your story is not always easy. Should you go to your church? In the next chapter we will consider how to find spiritual support as a victim of abuse. Should you go to a community agency? In chapter four we consider the various forms of help available in the community. But it is critical that you go somewhere. Do not keep silent about what is happening in your home. You need to tell someone. Tell them soon.

Where to go first is something that you alone will need to decide. In the pages to follow, we look at some of the factors you'll need to consider as you make this decision. Sometimes a church is not a safe place to disclose that you have been a victim of abuse. Sometimes a community agency or a shelter is not a safe place to talk about your faith in God or your love of the church. That means you will need to look at more than one place for help as you chart out your healing journey. Sadly, many Christian women keep their abuse a tightly guarded secret. And what maintains their silence? Fear.

For Spiritual Reflection

Like many other women, she had waited too long to disclose her tragic secret. Now, to save her children, she had to reveal her desperate situation. Her anxiety made her stumble as she made her way on legs stiffened by reluctance. The prophet's widow had chosen Elisha as her best resource, seeking a spiritual counselor as many others do. Would the revelation reflect badly on her husband? Would Elisha accuse her of lack of faith or not managing her household well?

Her husband's death had left her with few resources, and she was unused to handling the family finances. She couldn't repay her debts, and now one of the creditors was about to seize her two precious sons as slaves. They would remain in bondage all their lives, until the year of Jubilee. When she reached Elisha, she told the story quickly: "Your servant my husband is dead; and you know that your servant feared the Lord, but a creditor has come to take my two children as slaves" (2 Kings 4:1).

Elisha does not offer her money to solve the problem. Instead he directs her to use her own resources and those of her neighbors. His questioning soon reveals that she has nothing in her house except one small jar of oil. Like Hagar, she will find a way to use what is already at hand. Since she has no other containers, she must borrow a large quantity of empty jars from her friends and neighbors. This will be a time of community sharing, not of secrecy but of support. In the end the borrowed containers will be returned, but first they must be used as part of her deliverance.

As Elisha has instructed, the widow returns home, borrows the containers, takes them into her house with her two boys and shuts the door. The community has been helpful, but there is work that she must do for herself. She is to pour her oil into each of the containers that she and her sons have collected.

As the children bring one jar after another, she fills each with oil from her little jar. On and on she works, pouring the oil that will save her family from slavery and debt. Finally, with her own little pot still brimming, she calls for one more jar; but all of them are already full. And then the miraculous flow stops.

She joyously bursts out of her home to share the news not only with Elisha but with all the neighbors who helped her. Again Elisha guides her. "Go sell the oil and pay your debts, and you and your children can live on the rest" (2 Kings 4:7). Again she will be responsible for managing her family's resources, now delivered from the terrible fear that had threatened her children's safety and well-being. She has discovered the blessing of spiritual counsel, the help of others and guidance in being able to help herself. Most of all, she has learned that God's power can work in and through her.

The whole Bible is about God's deliverance from oppression. The great salvation event of the Old Testament is the freeing of the children of Israel from slavery and genocide in Egypt.

God declared to Moses, "I have observed the misery of my people who are in Egypt; I have heard their cry on account of their taskmasters. Indeed, I know their sufferings, and I have come down to deliver them from the Egyptians, and to bring them up out of that land to a good and broad land. . . . The cry of the Israelites has now come to me; I have also seen how the Egyptians oppress them" (Exodus 3:7-9; see also vv. 16-17). Just as God had seen and heard Hagar, so now he saw and heard the Israelites.

The rescue did not happen all at once, and many of the children of Israel were at first unwilling to believe. But at last the miracle came. The people left Egypt and marched on dry land through the Red Sea. Israel was delivered from a seemingly hopeless situation, and the people were truly free.

After that, God's goodness, power, loving attention and provision were remembered. The exodus, the setting free of a slave people, became the defining event in Israel's history. Later there were other defining moments as the Israelites crossed the wilderness and vowed to be his people as he would be their God. They entered the Promised Land as a free people who had experienced real encounters with the Lord their God. Whenever moral and spiritual failure led them into oppression from other enemies, God raised up deliverers (Judges

2:16) and marvelous means of deliverance.

The Bible is full of stories of individuals who were saved from bondage, degradation and abuse. Again and again the Scriptures express God's desire to set free those who are oppressed and assaulted, and to give them a new identity (Isaiah 62:2-4).

> *For you, O God, tested us;*
> *you refined us like silver.*
> *You brought us into prison*
> *and laid burdens on our backs.*
> *You let people ride over our heads;*
> *we went through fire and water,*
> *but you brought us to a place of abundance.*
> *(Psalm 66:10-12 British NIV)*

How similar is this to what some women have suffered. Kept as prisoners in their own homes, cut off from friends and family, physically, mentally and sexually abused, they have indeed gone "through fire and water."

God's place of abundance is waiting for those courageous enough to find it. That can be hard to believe if you have been oppressed and have not been taught that you are an heir of God's kingdom. But there is a place of healing and restoration of identity. This is God's promise, and God is faithful and true.

Three

WHERE DO I FIND
SPIRITUAL SUPPORT?

ONE COOL OCTOBER DAY A GROUP OF MEN AND WOMEN assembled for a church history workshop. Unlike many gatherings where I make a presentation, this day was not devoted specifically to a discussion of abuse or to how the church should respond to the needs of those in crisis. Instead its focus was intellectual, and those who gathered were mostly people intrigued by ideas.

During the lunch that followed my presentation, a petite woman approached me and asked in a gentle voice. "Could we talk for a minute?" Before I even had a chance to nod, she continued, "I think you might be interested in my story." These are words I have come to appreciate more and more as I have had opportunities to speak publicly about violence.

We sat down at an empty table, amid the noise of nearly one hundred people getting their lunches and exercising their voices after hours of listening to speakers. Mary began to open the floodgates. "I was married to a clergyman," she began.

Over a number of years her husband had repeatedly struck her body and hurled harsh words at her spirit. Eventually Mary fled the rectory where she lived and went to the battered women's shelter in a neighboring community. Here she found a group of women who understood the violence she had endured, were sympathetic to her need for a safe place to live, but were unable to understand why faith was important or the beauty she found in the traditions of the church. Her physical needs were cared for well by the shelter and its staff, but Mary's spirit continued to bleed.

The longer we talked, the more her questions surfaced: Didn't anybody in the church care why she had disappeared? Why didn't anyone look for her? How did her husband explain her absence? What did the church have to offer her when she was in need? Where was God in her suffering?

By chance one day, Mary was walking a few blocks from the women's shelter when she came face to face with the bishop who supervised her husband and was responsible for the well-being of his congregation. Although the bishop did not seem interested in talking with her, Mary cornered him, peppering him with questions. "Did you know that I was living in the transition house? Do you know why women flee to transition houses? Why didn't you come to visit me?"

As Mary told me what the bishop had said, tears came to her eyes and mine. The bishop didn't want to be seen at a battered women's shelter. The bishop didn't want to see her. The bishop didn't want to believe that her husband, a parish priest, was violent. So the bishop had taken the path of least resistance. *Refuse to look at the wounds. Pretend they don't exist. Turn the other way.* He responded like the priest and the Levite in the story of the good Samaritan.

Though many years had passed since her days in the battered women's shelter, she was still in pain because church leaders had ignored her plight. Turning a blind eye does not erase the pain or the long-term impact of the abuse. And the pain and the impact of abuse can extend well beyond the family itself.

You know there are spiritual needs deep within when you say to yourself . . .

Where is God in the midst of my suffering?

Has God given up on me?

Doesn't God care?

What did I do to deserve this?

I am a bad person; there is no hope for me.

Since I was a child, I have disappointed those around me.

Nobody loves me.

My parents said I was stupid. They're right.

I must not be a Christian if this is happening to me.

I promised God that I would stay with him, for better, for worse.

Maybe if I had prayed more often for my husband, he wouldn't have hit me.

Is God trying to teach me a lesson through all of my suffering?

I will be condemned to hell if I get divorced.

The counselor at the shelter thinks my religion is responsible for the abuse.

How can I ever face people in the church again?

I want my kids to believe we are a happy Christian family.

If I leave my husband, will the children ever forgive me?

Can I still sing on the praise team if I'm divorced?

Spiritual Issues Related to Abuse

Like Mary, you may have some aching spiritual needs as you begin to re-
build your life after saying no to abuse. While the staff at most shelters
and transition houses are trained to respond to the emergency needs of
women and children seeking shelter, they often don't know how to
counsel women about their journey of faith. This leaves many abused
Christian women feeling torn between their commitment to God and the
church and the support and help of counselors and community agencies. You may have already felt this conflict if you have sought help from
people outside of your faith community.

As you journey toward wholeness, you will find that your struggle has
spiritual dimensions. These spiritual concerns can either help or hinder
you. There are questions and needs that have to be resolved. When you
seek help for resolving these deep struggles, your faith will be a great resource in your healing journey. If you try to ignore or minimize them,
the journey can be far more difficult.

Who can help you think through all the spiritual questions that arise
in the midst of your suffering? Who can help you sort through your guilt
feelings? Who can point you to what the Bible says about protecting your
own safety and your children's? Normally only a person with pastoral
training—a minister or other religious leader—will be able to tease apart
the questions that nag your conscience. Such a person can help you see
when you have misunderstood the Bible's teachings about suffering,
faithfulness and patience.

We use the phrase "the language of the spirit" to talk about spiritual
help that is based on scriptural principles and rooted in a faith community. For the believer who has been abused, the language of the spirit has
to come alongside the language of contemporary culture in the healing
journey.

If you seek help from a professional therapist or from staff at a community agency or battered women's shelter, you may feel pressure to
downplay or hide your identity as a believer. You may be concerned that

Some of the questions and feelings that arise for a woman of faith who suffers abuse

abandonment: *Where is God now?*

beliefs about the Christian life: *What does God expect of believers?*

beliefs about marriage: *I promised for better, for worse.*

beliefs about divorce: *Is divorce an option for Christians?*

attempts to find meaning: *What did I do to deserve this?*

staff members who do not share your religious beliefs will think the abuse happened *because* you are a Christian. You may want to shelter your church from criticism or to protect yourself from unsympathetic questions about your commitment as a believer.

This means that battered women of faith, like you, are cautious about how much of their story they should tell and to whom. In church circles, you may minimize the impact of the abuse. In the shelter environment, you may keep your faith secret. Sometimes a victimized woman chooses to keep hidden the religious beliefs of her abuser.

Secular resources tell us that all abused women need to take charge of their own lives as they respond to the impact of violence and abuse. But for women with little money and with very low self-esteem, this is very, very hard.

By contrast, the language of the spirit speaks of healing and of connecting with God and with sisters and brothers in God's family. But for women who believe that they have failed in their marriage, this too is very, very hard.

Yet when the resources of contemporary culture and the spiritual world are brought together, believers who have suffered abuse, like you, are given strength and support to combat even the greatest of fears.

Abandonment. You may feel that God has abandoned you in your time of need. You may feel all alone, cut off from friends and family, separated like a goat from the sheep within the flock of the good Shepherd.

Every abused woman feels abandoned and afraid. But for a Christian woman who believes that God is ever-present, this is especially painful. These feelings reinforce the guilt you feel about the problems in your marriage. You may feel responsible to make your husband happy, manage his tension and keep the relationship stable.

A pastor or another religious leader can speak directly to these feelings, maybe by reminding you of biblical characters who felt abandoned or by retelling Bible stories involving dysfunctional and abusive families.

Beliefs about the Christian life. You may feel that your experiences of abuse have pushed you to the margins of what Christian family living is supposed to be. Thus you feel both guilt and a sense of being trapped—there seems little you can do to make things change.

To counter confusion about the Christian life, a pastor can help you think about who God really is. He or she will help you ask important questions: Would the God you worship want you to be in a relationship with somebody who is verbally and physically abusive? Does God want people to live in unhealthy relationships with no peace or stability?

Questions like these will help you to examine your circumstances in light of what God is really like. They will help you see how different God's desire for families is from the abuse you are enduring. In fact, peace and tranquility in the home are central to biblical teaching on godly families (see appendix two).

Beliefs about marriage. A pastor is the appropriate person to respond to the anxiety you feel about your promise before God to love and care for your husband "for better, for worse." In fact, our research showed that often an abuse victim who finally decides to look for help finds a way to talk with the minister or priest who married her—even if she or he lives far away. Perhaps she is seeking the pastor's permission to leave the abusive marriage. She may want to tell the minister what went wrong.

You too may feel that the beliefs you have held about marriage are about to be shattered. A wise pastor can help you see that you have not broken your promise; it is the man who abused you who has broken the marriage vow.

Beliefs about separation and divorce. Many Christian abuse victims agonize over whether divorce is an option for a believer. Perhaps you are struggling with this right now. Many pastors find it a very difficult issue too; they feel caught between their belief "marriage is forever" and the reality of violence in the home. In the words of one pastor, "I believe in the commitment of marriage and would want to fully max that out, but there are certain times when it becomes clear, it doesn't matter how much energy you put into it, it's that type of thing where separation is warranted. And I would counsel people in exactly that way."[1]

Many pastoral counselors point out that it is the violence that ends the relationship, not the victim's decision to leave. The victimized woman thus does not bear responsibility for the failure of the marriage. In the safety of his pastoral study, one minister offered this advice: "The Christian message of resurrection is one of new life. If situations or relationships have been dealt a death blow, surely new life must be a hope. To discern what is authentic new life is a matter to be grappled with, hopefully with one's pastor[al] counselor. In many cases, this new life will involve recognition that the relationship has died, and so divorce becomes the burial."[2]

The Old Testament made provision for a slave woman to divorce her master if he failed to give her food, clothing and love (Exodus 21:10-11). Jewish courts of law allowed free women the right to divorce on the same grounds.

The apostle Paul directed divorce to be allowed if an unbeliever wished to leave the marriage: "If the unbeliever leaves, let them leave. A brother or sister is not enslaved in such circumstances. God has called

Spiritual Elements of the Healing Journey

AWARENESS OF YOUR SUFFERING

Your experiences of abuse are shared by many women in our community, across the country and in every nation of the world. *You are not alone.*

Abuse happens in all kinds of families, among those who are believers and those who are not. *Abuse occurs in churchgoing families too.*

There are many Christians who want to help families in crisis but are not sure what to do. *You need to help others know how to help you.*

Many pastors have information on violence in the home; in fact, a flyer about abuse may have been put in the women's washroom of the church. *You need to get plenty of information about abuse, either from the church or from a community agency.*

CONDEMNATION OF THE ABUSIVE BEHAVIOR

Abuse is wrong, in any language, at any time, in any culture. *What happened to you is wrong. You are not to blame.*

The God we serve has condemned violence in the Scriptures. *God speaks out against violence in the Bible. Read it in the Word.*

Many churches and many faith groups stand firm against men battering women or women battering men. *Find out how your congregation supports violence-free family living.*

EMPATHY

There are people who would feel honored to hear what is happening in your life. *Feel free to call them and see if they are available, just to listen. Someday they may need to ask for your help.*

It will be very difficult for you to discuss your abuse. *Those who listen need to promise that they will keep your story confidential.*

You may face many practical needs. *What are some of the ways your church could help you now? Be sure to tell a church leader; otherwise they may not realize what help you need.*

YOUR IMMEDIATE NEEDS

You need to develop a safety plan. *Have you ever thought of putting copies of important documents, extra cash and telephone numbers of agencies in a safe place, in case you need to leave your home very quickly?*

In a moment of danger, you will need help. *Are you connected with someone in the church, or at the shelter, trained to assist someone in immediate danger?*

The police are trained to respond to a crisis call. *You can always call 911 or the local police directly if you are in urgent need of help.*

REFERRALS

Become aware of the resources available in your area to help hurting families. *Do you know about the agencies and programs in your community that might be able to help you?*

Know the name of the local shelter for battered women and how to get help there. *Keep the telephone number of the shelter in a safe place in case you ever want to talk to a worker there or in case you need to flee your house in a hurry.*

Ask whether there is an emergency response team at your church. *A pastor or a woman leader should be able to give you the names of one or two people who could assist you in a crisis.*

you to peace" (1 Corinthians 7:15). It is precisely when speaking of a stormy marriage situation that Paul says, "God has called you to peace." Some Christians believe his words apply only to the case of a believer married to an unbeliever. But Matthew 18:15-17 tells us to treat the unrepentant as unbelievers. So does 1 Timothy: "If anyone does not thoughtfully care for their own family, and especially those in their own household, they have denied the faith and are worse than an unbeliever" (1 Timothy 5:8).

Attempts to find meaning. In the aftermath of violence, many questions crowd the mind and heart of an abused woman. Sometimes you even wonder if the abuse is punishment from God. In the cry of one victim:[3] "Why is this happening? . . . I never did anything to deserve this. I've gone to church all my life. I've been trying to live a good life."

Maybe you have been asking yourself, *Am I being punished for something I did that was wrong?* Some victims point to a pregnancy before marriage, or an abortion, or premarital sexual intimacy as possible reasons God would punish them now. Other victims blame themselves, their own attitudes and behavior, for their husband's anger and violence.

Nobody deserves to be abused. Of course you haven't been perfect. Who has? Your task is to ask God to help you see where you've been wrong and where you are feeling false guilt. Remember that Satan is the one who accuses believers (Revelation 12:9-10); the Greek word for "devil" (*diabolos*) actually means "accuser."

When we are overcome with our past faults, we can't move forward into constructive action. The good news is that we are forgiven because of Christ's redemptive sacrifice for us. "He himself bore our sins in his body on the tree, so that, free from sins, we might live for righteousness" (1 Peter 2:24). God has called us to freedom. We have the right to be confident of being forgiven.

You may find that others are forcing you into a guilt trip. Abusers like to say, "It's all your fault," shifting the blame from themselves to you. Your load is too heavy already. Don't accept the blame for the violence. *No one deserves abuse.*

Sometimes, sadly, even church leaders will ask what you did to cause the abuse. They may find it hard to believe that your husband could be so nice at work and in church—he may even be a church leader!—and then behave so badly at home.

You need rich doses of God's grace to keep your head straight in the midst of all this. But safety and freedom from fear are promises from God. You must claim these divine promises as you go about seeking refuge from your partner's violence.

At each point in the healing journey, many Christian victims, just like you, have spiritual needs. For these needs to be met, they have to be understood. Amidst the crisis, your faith must be affirmed.

FOR SPIRITUAL REFLECTION

None of the biblical authors shares with us more intimately than David his sense of being mistreated and oppressed and his joy in finding God as his strength. His openness makes his writings especially helpful to women emerging from the dark shadows of abuse.

In the Psalms we find the most forthright condemnations of violence (Psalm 5:9; 7:1-2; 10:2, 7-10; 17:11; 27:12; 31:4, 10-13; 37:32; 38:11-12; 52:2-3; 54:3; 55:12-14, 20-21; 56:5-6; 59:3; 64:1-6; 69:4, 19-20; 86:14; 140:1-5), the most passionate appeals to God for deliverance (59:2; 139:19; 140:1, 4) and the deepest assurances of God's power to give safety and support (10:17-18; 12:5; 28:8-9; 34:6; 35:10; 103:6).

David's experiences forced him into acute and painful self-examination. When he was homeless and hunted, his cries went up to God. When he was relentlessly pursued by those who sought to kill him, he made his plight known to God. When he was stalked and vilified and in the depths of despair, God was there. When his words were twisted and he was taunted, he could still find his identity in God (Psalm 56:2, 5-6).

This is why the psalms of David are so important for the healing of wounded women. They are prayers that connect us to God, prayers that are sometimes disturbingly frank. He wonders if God has forgotten him, no longer cares about him, won't bother to listen. David dares to state his painful questions with complete honesty. He expresses his anger at the almighty Creator and waits for a response.

Again and again the answers come to him—God *is* there, God will bring deliverance after all. David maintains a sense of his own rectitude. Enemies have abused him, but he has been steadfast in serving God. The psalms that speak of his integrity can be of enormous help to women (Psalm 26:1-12; 41:12; 57:7; 101:2-7). He is sometimes in anguish because people he trusted have betrayed him (Psalm 55:20).

Some Christians find it hard to accept David's anger, his desire for vengeance on those who have harmed him. He displays excruciating honesty about his emotions, even the negative ones. Most of us are reluctant to express such hostility openly, but David's bitterness can be helpful to an abused woman who needs to vent her anger before she can really be healed.

A Christian woman who was struggling to forgive her husband's infidelity attended a ballet one evening. One dance represented the ancient story of Medea, a woman who sacrificed everything for love of her husband and later was betrayed by him. After helping Jason steal a golden fleece from her native land, Medea married him and bore him two sons. But Jason, ever the opportunist, decided to set her aside to marry the daughter of the king. The story is full of bitter rage and vindictive jealousy.

As the ballerina danced in writhing fury, the Christian woman in the audience entered into those feelings and felt herself cleansed of them. God used the artistic experience to bring her wholeness.

In the same way, even David's most angry and vengeful expressions can be used by the power of the Holy Spirit. Always David's meditations bring him back to God.

David, the ignored youngest son of Jesse, was anointed as a mere lad to be king of Israel. Although resented and ridiculed by his older brothers, he took on the challenge of single-handed combat with the champion of the Philistines who oppressed the land. With the terrible velocity of a sling-driven rock, he brought down the giant and gained the freedom of his people. He was brought into the king's court and had a brilliant military career that brought extravagant praise but roused the jealousy of King Saul, who became depressed and bitter.

At first David was able to calm the king by playing his harp. But soon it became clear that his life was in jeopardy. One day Saul threw a spear at him, and David was barely able to dodge the blade. Later Saul commanded his servants and his son to kill David, but he was helped to escape. Even the priests who gave him food were executed, and David understood that there was nowhere in Saul's kingdom where he could be safe.

He went first to the country of the Philistines, then to a cave in the wilderness. There he was joined by other men who had fallen out of favor with Saul. David and his band began providing services for Israelites there in the wilderness, especially the farmers and shepherds who were being threatened by bandits.

But the insanely jealous Saul continued to hunt David. One day Saul went into a cave to relieve himself. It happened that David was hiding farther back in the cave, and he crept up and cut off a piece of Saul's garment. He could easily have killed him, but instead David followed the king out of the cave and showed him the piece of cloth, demonstrating that he meant Saul no harm. At first the king repented of the evil that he had planned (1 Samuel 24:16-22), but soon he returned to his old ways (26:2) and again sought David's life. This time, as Saul lay sleeping, David removed the spear and water jug that lay beside his head. Waking up and realizing that David had again spared his life, the king again vowed repentance (26:21-25).

Though the words were impressive, the reality was lacking. Saul's search widened, and David was forced to move from place to place, always in hiding, always fearful that he would be betrayed. He was compelled not only to change his location but to provide resources for his family and for the growing group of refugees who sought shelter with him.

In many ways David's experiences paralleled those of an endangered woman. Direct attempts were made on his life, his only safety lay in staying hidden, and some people betrayed his whereabouts (see Psalm 52 and 1 Samuel 22:9-10). His devotion to the king and years of faithful service were met with hostility and treachery. He who had been the captain of Saul's bodyguard now found the army turned against him.

So it was that he wrote:

> All who hate me whisper together about me;
>> they imagine the worst for me. . . .
> Even my bosom friend in whom I trusted,
>> who ate of my bread, has lifted his heel against me. (Psalm 41:7, 9)

Lies were being told about him.

> For I hear the whispering of many—
>> terror all around!—
> as they scheme together against me,
>> as they plot to take my life. (Psalm 31:13)

The abused woman may not be as eloquent as the sweet singer of Israel, but she can understand the pain of betrayal by one whom she loved and trusted. David knew too what it is to be stalked.

> The wicked watch for the righteous,
>> and seek to kill them.
> The LORD will not abandon them to their power,
>> or let them be condemned when they are brought to trial.
> (Psalm 37:32-33)

You may find great strength in meditating on the songs of David. You can use them as prayers when you are too distraught to offer prayers of your own. You can find comfort in them when few are willing to believe your story or offer you support. You may wish to compile a list of readings that you can return to again and again in times of need.

A number of psalms are related to specific experiences in the life of David.

Psalm 3 expresses his emotions when he has been betrayed by his own son Absalom, who has raised up an insurrection against him and is seeking to seize the throne. In God alone is his hope.

Psalm 31 grieves not only his danger and desperation but that his old friends and acquaintances have turned upon him. Christ quoted from this psalm when he was dying on the cross (see Psalm 31:5). Yet David finds God's presence even in the worst of his misery.

> *I will exult and rejoice in your steadfast love,*
> > *because you have seen my affliction;*
> > *you have taken heed of my adversities,*
> *and have not delivered me into the hand of the enemy;*
> > *you have set my feet in a broad place.* (Psalm 31:7-8)

What better prayer could be uttered by a woman on the road to healing?

Psalms 34 and 56 are based on a time when David was desperately seeking a place where he might stay in safety (see 1 Samuel 21:10-15). Finding no place among his friends and kin, he went to the Philistine king of Gath. It was an enormous risk, but he had few options. The king's servants recognized him as an enemy, and now his life was in even greater jeopardy. Quickly he pretended to be insane. He gouged his fingernails into the city gate and let his spit run down on his beard. So he was driven away as a madman and made his escape to a remote cave.

The need to flee for one's life, to find quick solutions for desperate situations, are all part of David's prayer experience. If you have had to resort to deception in order to escape from abuse, you will identify with him.

Psalm 51 is the most famous, his confession after the sin of adultery with Bathsheba and murder of her husband. His profound repentance still sets an example for all who sin.

Psalm 52 rings with agony over those who have been killed as punishment for having helped him with shelter, food, weapons and spiritual counsel (see 1 Samuel 21:1-9; 22:9-23). In Saul's fury, the whole priestly community was exterminated, with the exception of Abiathar, who served as David's chaplain and continued to seek the Lord on David's behalf.

Psalm 54 was written on the occasion of another betrayal when David was desperately seeking a place to hide from Saul (see 1 Samuel 23:15-26; 26:1). He was living in the desert with his family and those who had come to him for help. He thought he had found safety in the wilderness of Ziph, and there his dear friend Jonathan visited him for one last time. But the citizens of Ziph, seeking to curry favor with the king, notified Saul of his whereabouts. Worse yet, they promised, "Come down whenever it pleases you to do so, and we will be responsible for handing him over to the king" (1 Samuel 23:20). His neighbors had turned traitor, but God was still faithful.

Psalm 55 has no inscription about the occasion on which it was written, but it contains a section that is often used for meditation by those who have known abuse by an intimate partner.

> It is not enemies who taunt me—
>   I could bear that;
> it is not adversaries who deal insolently with me—
>   I could hide from them.
> But it is you, my equal,
>   my companion, my familiar friend,
> with whom I kept pleasant company;
>   we walked in the house of God with the throng. (Psalm 55:12-14)

Psalm 57 is another song of escape: "In the shadow of your wings I will take refuge until the destroying storms pass by" (v. 1). Psalm 59 was composed when Saul sent assassins to watch David's house in order to execute him. Psalm 60 is written after a military defeat, and Psalm 63 gives his thoughts while he is a refugee in the desert of Judah.

When David was at last delivered from all of his enemies and from Saul, he sang.

In my distress I called upon the LORD;
to my God I called.
From his temple he heard my voice,
and my cry came to his ears. . . .
He reached from on high, he took me,
he drew me out of mighty waters.
He delivered me from my strong enemy,
from those who hated me;
for they were too mighty for me.
They came upon me in the day of my calamity;
but the LORD was my stay.
He brought me out into a broad place;
he delivered me, because he delighted in me. (2 Samuel 22:7, 17-20)

Reading David's songs prayerfully allows us to share vicariously the bitterness, resentment, sense of betrayal and outrage that he feels. If you are struggling to forgive, this can lead to a release of your own emotions. These psalms give us permission to experience the pain and then to move on, as David does. His anger is vehement and bitter, but his delight in God is glorious as he moves into God's deliverance. He exults in the Savior who has brought him to a new place and given him a new song.

The psalms of David might form a special prayer book for abused women, one you might use in your own spiritual recovery. You can pray them in your devotions or use them to sing praise, exulting in God's abundant grace. You too will find the "broad place" of which David speaks.

You are a hiding place for me;
you preserve me from trouble;
you surround me with glad cries of deliverance. (Psalm 32:7)

WHAT HELP CAN I FIND
IN THE COMMUNITY?

WHEN YOU FIRST THINK ABOUT IT, the idea that pastors, police, shelter workers, lawyers, therapists and counselors would work together on the issue of abuse in Christian families—families like yours—sounds like a recipe for disaster. Wouldn't there be conflicting advice? What if you felt pulled between your faith and your freedom? What if the community agency and its personnel argue against the advice of the church?

These are logical questions to ask until you consider how many layers there are to abuse. No one agency has all the services to meet your needs. No one professional has all the answers required for the journey into healing and wholeness. Actually collaboration and coordination between those who want to assist a battered woman are the most reasonable approach.

As an abused woman you may need police protection, just as much as your neighbor. You may need to talk to a therapist, consult a lawyer, seek shelter in a transition house, or call the school for advice about your children's educational and emotional needs. At some point you may require medical attention and perhaps longer-term psychotherapy or counseling.

So though you are a Christian, you will need the help of secular service providers. The church can't deal with family violence in isolation from other community services. And most often it will be up to you to find and use these resources.

However, as a battered *Christian* woman, you will also need spiritual help and guidance as you look at what has taken place in your marriage, evaluate your options and begin reconstructing your life. In addition to the emotional and practical problems you must tackle, you will have spiritual questions and concerns as you journey from victim to survivor.

The assistance you'll need involves both the language of contemporary culture—from trained professionals in law, medicine, psychology, psychiatry and social work—and the language of the spirit. As the previous chapters in this book have emphasized, the Bible is far from silent on the issue of abuse. "Again I saw all the oppressions that are practiced under the sun. Look, the tears of the oppressed—with no one to comfort them! On the side of their oppressors there was power—with no one to comfort them" (Ecclesiastes 4:1). "The LORD saw it, and it displeased him that there was no justice. He saw that there was no one, and was appalled that there was no one to intervene" (Isaiah 59:15-16). "Whoever winks the eye causes trouble, but the one who rebukes boldly makes peace" (Proverbs 10:10). Violent and controlling acts are condemned, and believers are admonished to live in peace and harmony within their homes. "Seek peace, and pursue it" (Psalm 34:14; 1 Peter 3:11). "Let us then pursue what makes for peace and for mutual upbuilding" (Romans 14:19). "Blessed are the peacemakers, for they will be called children of God" (Matthew 5:9).

In evangelical circles we hear much talk about God's pattern for family living, but we often fail to notice that much of what the Bible says about home life has to do with peace, safety and security. "My people will abide in a peaceful habitation, in secure dwellings, and in quiet resting places" (Isaiah 32:18). The repeated promise in Scripture is that there will be peace, safety and freedom from terror in the home of the godly.

"They shall live in safety, and no one shall make them afraid" (Ezekiel 34:28). "You shall know that your tent is safe" (Job 5:24). Within their own homes, God's people should be able not only to lie down in safety (Leviticus 26:6; Psalm 3:6; Isaiah 14:30; Jeremiah 23:6; 32:37; 33:16; Hosea 2:18) but also to live in safety (Jeremiah 34:24-28; Ezekiel 28:26; 34:24-28; 38:8). Isaiah is even more explicit:

> Your children shall be taught by the LORD,
>   and great shall be the prosperity of your children.
> In righteousness you shall be established;
>   you shall be far from oppression, for you shall not fear;
>   and from terror, for it shall not come near you.
> If anyone stirs up strife,
>   it is not from me;
> whoever stirs up strife with you
>   shall fail because of you. . . .
> No weapon that is fashioned against you shall prosper,
>   and you shall confute every tongue that rises against you in
>   judgment.
> This is the heritage of the servants of the LORD
>   and their vindication from me, says the LORD (Isaiah 54:13-14, 17)

Hold fast to this promise.

To be sure, when abuse exists, there is no peace. So the call to those in danger is to flee, to seek safety and respite, and to protect the weakest and most vulnerable, their children (Luke 23:29). "Then those in Judea must flee to the mountains, and those inside the city must leave it, and those out in the country must not enter it. . . . Woe to those who are pregnant and to those who are nursing infants!" (Luke 21:21, 23).

The language of the spirit is communicated by the written word, spoken through the weekly services of the church, reinforced by the tender tugging of God's Spirit at our hearts and minds, and practiced when believers show compassion to one another.

Who speaks the language of the spirit with authority? First and foremost, it is pastors who are trained in biblical knowledge and devotion, spiritually attuned, attempting to live close to the heart of God and eager to help others do likewise. Added to the pastors are many laypeople, women and men who love God and want to give Christ's love to others. By their acts of mercy, they bridge the chasm between a holy God and a hurting world.

THE POWER OF CARING ACTION

The mayor's office in Calgary, Alberta, a city in western Canada, sponsors a yearly campaign to reduce family violence, called "Turn Off the Violence." During this one week in November there is a concerted effort to highlight woman abuse, child abuse, elder abuse and other kinds of family violence. There are activities for schoolchildren, such as "Draw a picture that represents what 'Turn Off the Violence' means to you." Everything is aimed at breaking the silence surrounding abuse, making the community a safer place for a victim to say, "This has happened to me," and making sure there are community resources to deal with the emotional and practical needs of victims and their families.

Talks about abuse are given in churches, in hotels and in boardrooms. Judges, social workers, police, shelter staff, probation officers and clergy gather to reflect on the services they provide to victims of abuse or the perpetrators of violence. They ask questions like these: What help do victims require, and how best can we meet their needs? How can we coordinate our activities to serve people better and reduce violence in our community? Can we reduce overlap in the services provided and broaden the options for those in need?

Just inside the door of a battered women's shelter in Calgary, the walls are covered with color. Bright quilts stretch over the institutional walls to create a warm, inviting atmosphere. They were created and donated by a group of elderly church women who wanted to express care for the women who had fled to the shelter because they were too fearful to go home. Using needles and thread, these "grannies" offered gifts, not of gold, frankincense and myrrh, but of stitches, fragments of cloth and designs that are pleasing to the eye. In this way they built a bridge between

Signs that my church is a safe place to disclose that I am a battered woman

In the women's washroom there is information about local shelters or transition houses and how I can contact them.

My pastor has preached a sermon in which abuse was condemned and violence-free family living was celebrated.

The topic of battered women has been discussed sympathetically in the women's Bible study or in Sunday school.

There are brochures in the church foyer or outside the pastor's office that deal explicitly with the problem of abuse.

Support groups are available for abused women, either within the church or by referral.

A community leader involved with abuse has spoken at a church-sponsored function.

The topic of violence was raised by the pastor in the classes or premarital counseling sessions we attended before our wedding.

On Mother's Day there is explicit reference to the fact that many women live in fear, in homes where their safety cannot be taken for granted.

There have been fundraising efforts at my church for a local battered women's shelter.

their church and the shelter, saying without uttering a sound, *We care; God cares.*

You may not live in Calgary, but there are many women and men in your community and in your church who are committed to your needs as an abused woman. Some offer tangible support, or would be willing to do so if called upon, and some with more public confidence name the issue of abuse and declare openly their support for transition houses for families in crisis. Take heart as you muster the courage to look for help.

Whether professionals are discussing how to work together to assist a battered woman, or whether we are thinking creatively with an abused mother about her next move, one of the first steps is *breaking the silence.* In a church, an important question must be asked: is our church a safe place to disclose that one is a victim of abuse? In a secular service organization, the question would be, are community agencies safe places to disclose that one is a Christian? The answer to both questions *should* be yes. In any community, the answer to one or both questions may be "sometimes," or even more disturbing, "not really."

UNDERSTANDING COMMUNITY RESOURCES

Coordination between the agencies that serve battered women sounds a lot easier than it is in practice. But there is a growing recognition that co-ordination is in the best interests of those seeking help.

The victim needs to know what services she can expect from different community agencies and professionals. *Legal advice* will help to answer these kinds of questions: Can I get assistance to require my abusive husband to leave our home temporarily? What is the process for obtaining a restraining order? If I flee our home for several days or a few weeks, can he prevent me from returning? What is the difference between a legal separation and a certificate of divorce? Who decides custody of the children if I pursue the option of a divorce?

If there are wounds and injuries from an attack, *medical attention* may

What is it like to stay in a shelter?

A shelter offers safety rather than deluxe accommodations.
When Jacob was forced to flee for his life, he found himself
sleeping upon the hard ground with a stone for a pillow.
Yet there God appeared to him and promised to be with
him. To his amazement, Jacob saw a vision of a ladder
reaching up to heaven with angels ascending and
descending. You can find that ladder in the women's shelter,
for God is there, promising to be with you wherever you go
(Genesis 28:10-21).

*A shelter is usually less comfortable than your own home
but offers far better security.* Often its address is not public
in order to give better protection, and you may be
instructed never to tell the location so that the residents
and staff can remain safe. The elaborate system of locks,
buzzers, closed-circuit TV, intercom and so forth may seem
a bit intimidating, but they are there to protect you.

*Inside the shelter, the quarters may be cramped because so
many women need to be housed.* You and your children will
be assigned to a room, and you will find yourself part of a
community with other women and children. Usually the
residents take turns cooking and doing cleanup and other
tasks. There will be guidelines about using the telephone so
that you do not put the shelter at risk. The staff will be able
to devise ways of letting your family know that you are safe
and being cared for.

*Sometimes children, especially older ones, have trouble
adjusting to the shelter.* Sometimes there is an attractive
lounge area, with games and activities for adolescents;

sometimes there is not enough space. For younger children, there are normally daycare facilities, often with a fine staff of caregivers. If it can be arranged safely, your children may still attend school, and you may even be able to continue working. Perhaps you can park in a different space at work, or arrive and leave your job at new times. You and your children need to be careful not to return to the same stores, bank and post office that you had been using.

Frequently the shelter is already full. In this case you may be placed first in a private home, a "safe house." Again, it is important never to reveal the address of a safe house, as this may endanger you or the family who offers you their hospitality. Sometimes it may be necessary for you to go to a facility that is not in your own community.

The staff at the shelter includes experienced counselors, many of whom have their own stories of abuse. Shelter workers have helped many abused women and are very familiar with resources, options and programs available in your area. They have walked women just like you through the very same kinds of crises and have helped them emerge stronger for it. Actually you can get this counseling without entering the shelter. The hotline is normally available twenty-four hours a day.

What if I still don't feel safe? In some cases a woman truly is not safe despite all the protection that the law and the shelter may try to offer. Experienced counselors can point out lifesaving options, such as moving to another part of the country or changing your name and social security number.

be needed right away. But a doctor's help may also be sought to document how much physical abuse you have suffered and how severe it has been. These are some of the questions you may want to address to a physician: Would you list for me the nature and extent of the injuries I have received? Can I expect full recovery? For how long should I expect to be under the care of a physician for my injuries? How has living in an abusive home affected my physical health?

The *police* are often the first to be called when a woman needs immediate protection from a violent partner. Today many police departments are training certain officers to respond to the needs of women and children in domestic crisis. Some questions you may wish to ask the police include these: What are the steps for having a violent partner removed from my home? Do I have to press charges against my abusive husband if I call 911? What happens after charges are filed? Do restraining orders really stop abusive husbands from endangering the lives of their wives and children?

Many victims require some *psychological therapy* after suffering violent acts. There may be layers of emotional pain, fear, guilt, anger and lots of questions related to how your mental and emotional health can be restored. A psychologist or psychiatrist can offer you help to address issues like these: Are there signs of poor emotional functioning in my own life or that of my children? How can I begin to restore faith in myself and control over my choices? How can I deal with the feelings of hopelessness and despair that seem to overcome me? What combination of medications and counseling would be most appropriate in my case? What strategies can I use to put the past behind me?

Often an abused woman has many questions about managing financially after she has left the abusive relationship. A *social worker* can guide you through the steps required to obtain temporary benefits from the state, such as welfare or food vouchers. Questions related to low-income housing, the waiting period for benefit payment, and job training programs for women who have never worked outside the home are all appropriate issues to be raised with a social worker.

Transition houses, or women's shelters, offer temporary housing for abused women. Normally the maximum length of stay is between six weeks and six months. If the local shelter is full, you and your children may be placed somewhere else until space opens up at the transition house. A number of shelters have community outreach workers who are available to talk to you over the phone or to visit your home by appointment. Shelters do not charge rent, but most require that residents help with meal preparation and cleanup. Many shelters have programs for children, and most have extensive connections to other agencies to assist you in meeting your emotional, legal and long-term housing needs. Some communities have second-stage housing as well, so you can move from the shelter to an apartment where you can stay for up to two years.

Support groups or community advocacy groups for victims have expanded greatly across North America in recent years. Sometimes these are organized by a mental health clinic or hospital. In groups like these, women come together on a regular basis (every two weeks or once a month) to discuss problems and solutions and to gain support from others who have also endured abuse. It's a good opportunity to give and receive ideas that help in the struggle of daily living. Sometimes these groups get the help of a professionally trained adviser; other times they are run solely by volunteers.

There is not often a concerted effort to encourage coordination and cooperation between churches and secular agencies in response to the needs of a Christian woman or family in crisis. Why? Partly because most professionals don't understand the spiritual elements of the healing journey for Christians. And secular professionals do not have a good understanding of the pastor's role in the situation; sometimes ministers themselves don't know how much they are needed!

WHAT KIND OF ASSISTANCE MIGHT MY PASTOR OFFER ME?
Here are some ideas you can bring to your pastor or spiritual mentor at this point of crisis in your life.

Help me to reflect on the nature of God . . .

- Affirm that God is always present with me.

- Remind me that God cares about human misery.

- Teach me to meditate on the value God places on human life.

- Assure me of how important my life is to God.

Help me to reflect on my need of God . . .

- On this earth, Jesus looked to God for strength. Teach me to do likewise.

- Reveal to me that our experience of weakness opens the door for God's help.

- When human resources have been exhausted, many men and women naturally look for God to intervene. Teach me to see this in a positive light.

- Suggest ways that I can look to God for strength.

Help me reflect on God's ability to meet my needs . . .

- Help me to cry out to God for strength.

- Help me to pray for courage.

- Suggest Bible passages that speak of God's provision in the midst of crises.

- Teach me to meditate on how God is sufficient to meet my personal needs.

Help me to condemn abuse using the language of the Spirit . . .

- Use the Bible's language to condemn the violence I have endured.

- Use the language of my faith tradition to condemn the violence I have endured.

- Use all the resources available within our congregation to condemn the violence I have endured.

- Teach *me* to condemn the violence I have endured.

Affirm the use of secular resources . . .

- Help me to see that it's wise to seek counsel from experts, even those who don't share my Christian faith.

- Point me to some specific community resources.

- Stay involved in supporting my healing journey even after I get help from some community-based services.

Offer me supportive services from church people . . .

- Connect me to persons and groups in our church able to respond to needs like mine.

- Offer me a listening ear so that I can talk about the pain I feel.

- Suggest any specific help our congregation has for people in crisis.

- Provide ongoing spiritual contact for me through both regular church events and spontaneous activities.

- In time, when I am ready, offer me ministry opportunities so that I can give support to others.

LOOKING FOR HELP

Abuse is ugly in any form and wrong in any context. Since it involves betrayal and humiliation, often it leaves the woman with little sense of self-worth. You have no doubt blamed yourself for the violence you have suffered, and maybe you still cling to the hope that the relationship will improve and the violence will stop. Like many abused women, you probably feel trapped, isolated and guilt-ridden.

Being a Christian, you said your marriage vows believing your promise was meant to last *forever,* until death ended it. Beyond that, Bible verses about forgiving may have propelled you into a cycle of hope followed by humiliation and despair. Some women even believe that abuse is their cross to bear. Women committed to Christ tend to feel extra guilt and extra pressure to "make the marriage work."

Getting the Services You Need and Deserve

BUILDING BLOCKS	
Safety, the first priority	The police and transition houses are best equipped to provide safety.
Long-term commitment to help	Services for your social and emotional needs fit into this category. Churches may play an important role in offering help on a longer-term basis.
Assisting in the journey, but not directing it	Legal services, school-based services, and the help of a doctor, psychologist or psychiatrist are often needed for a period of time.
THE CEMENT	
Establishing shared vision	Professionals sometimes work together to assist in a coordinated way. You can request this.
Recognizing areas of strength and diversity	In some ways it will be up to you to decide what forms of help you need and which professionals in your community can offer you assistance. Just as women differ from one another, so too do their needs in rebuilding their lives after abuse.
Building relationships between agencies	You can ask your pastor or agency staff for referral sources. Coordination works best when there is some established connection between the staff of the agencies.

When you think about it, it's easy to see why *secular* professionals might find it very hard, and sometimes frustrating, to work with clients whose religious beliefs are very strong. For sure, battered women who are Christians have some special therapeutic needs as they seek recovery and wholeness. For example, Christian women need to hear the violence condemned by their spiritual leader; this has a powerful impact, one that can't normally be produced in a social work office, a shelter or the police station.

Too often well-meaning (but ill-informed) healthcare professionals counsel battered Christian women to abandon their faith as they search for mental and physical well-being. Others simply ignore or underesti-mate a family's religious needs. Both of these responses are wrong. Instead religious and secular caregivers need to expand their referral networks to include each other.

A secular counselor needs to recognize your faith as a resource to help you deal with pain and an essential ingredient in your healing journey. At the same time, churches and religious leaders must never underestimate your need for money, food, safety, shelter, and practical advice and support.

Obviously, you as the client are not responsible for coordinating the services of various agencies! Still, there are certain measures you can take that might encourage communication and cooperation between the various service providers and thus improve the service you receive.

1. Identify the forms of assistance you are currently receiving.

2. As much as you are able, clarify the kinds of assistance you now need.

3. Ask for referral suggestions.

4. Identify what forms of assistance a person is able or willing to offer.

5. Clarify the cost of the service and how long you will need to wait before your appointment.

6. Give feedback (positive or negative) on services to the person who gave you the referral.

7. Don't hesitate to seek another source of help if you are not satisfied with the services you're being given.

8. When you feel it would be helpful, ask various service providers to make contact with each other. (They may ask you to fill out a consent form giving them permission to discuss your situation with someone else.)

9. Keep your expectations realistic. Service providers are often over-worked and may be working in agencies where funding is inadequate.

TAKING THE NEXT STEP

Shattering the silence on abuse is very important. Sometimes that silence is shattered as victims begin to ask questions of themselves or of their pastors or other counselors. Here are some questions you might be asking yourself as a Christian woman who has suffered abuse.

Would it indicate lack of faith if I were to develop a safety plan? Actually the Bible has a lot to say about being prepared, and it urges us to be watchful. While these things were said with reference to the Lord's return, they can be applied to other situations that call for caution and prudent foresight. Scripture is often fulfilled in more than one way. Preparing a safety plan is a loving and faithful thing to do. It may be the means of avoiding a terrible tragedy that could engulf your entire family. It can be a safeguard for the offender as well as for you and the children. Jesus says, "It will be good for those servants whose master finds them ready" (Luke 12:37 TNIV). "Keep awake therefore" (Matthew 24:42; see also Mark 13:35-37; Luke 12:40).

Does the Bible support me if I leave my home when I am frightened? Sometimes removing oneself is the safest course of action. In reference to perilous days to come Jesus taught: "Anyone on the housetop who has belongings in the house must not come down to take them away; and likewise anyone in the field should not turn back" (Luke 17:31). Jesus well understood the vulnerability of women and their responsibility to safeguard their children (Luke 23:28-29).

What should I tell my kids if I think the danger level is too high? Decide on a code word that will signal the children to go to their room and lock their door. One mother used the phrase "Power Rangers" to let the kids know that it was time to take cover. Is there a neighbor or relative nearby to whom they could go? Children need to understand that the first need is to secure their own safety rather than to worry about yours. Just as you might practice a fire drill, you can practice an emergency drill. Even a small child can be taught to dial 911 if there is danger.

What precautions should I take? Think carefully about how you might escape from the house if you needed to. What door or stairway would you use? Is there a window through which you could climb? Is there a neighbor's house to which you might run? Can you arrange a signal with a neighbor for when you need immediate help? Also, keep a list of important phone numbers where you can find them quickly. And put together an emergency kit.

What should I include in the emergency kit? Here's a helpful list from the Pennsylvania Coalition Against Domestic Violence:

- an extra set of car and house keys
- money, food stamps, checkbook, credit card(s), pay stubs
- birth certificates and other ID for you and your children
- your driver's license or other photo identification
- social security card or green card/work permit
- health insurance cards, medications for you and your children
- deed or lease to your house or apartment
- any court papers or orders
- change of clothes for you and your children

To this might be added a familiar toy for each child.

Make sure these things are ready in advance. Many women have been hurt or lost their lives returning home to get mail or other personal belongings. Tell as few people as possible about your plan to leave—only those who will be involved in your strategy. Leaving because of unsafe circumstances does not constitute legal desertion.

What if I change my mind? Most women who leave do so on a temporary basis, many in hopes that the abuse will stop. Some husbands realize the seriousness of the offense after the wife moves out. On average, women who actually separate permanently from their partner have attempted seven previous departures.

It *is* all right to change your mind if that seems the best plan. Frequently, unless the abuser is working very hard to change his ways, things fall back into the same pattern. The best strategy is to make sure that there's a structured change, not just empty promises. If he is going regularly to counseling or an intervention group for batterers, that's a good start.

Is it wrong to call 911? The Bible says that those who enforce the law are ministers of God, committed to justice (Romans 13:3-4). If you are injured, call 911 immediately to get medical help. Save any ripped or bloody clothes. Make sure that a doctor, nurse or friend takes pictures of your injuries and bruises. This is important evidence that you may need in the future. You can also call a twenty-four-hour domestic violence hotline for immediate help. Often volunteers from the shelter will accompany you to the emergency room.

Is it wrong to get a restraining order? Like dialing 911, a restraining order can save lives. It is not wrong to make use of the protection to which you are legally entitled. Legal intervention can be a help to both the victim and the perpetrator.

When police are called to a scene of domestic violence, they usually take the abuser with them to the station. Normally the detention lasts no longer than twenty-four hours, so you have only a short time to make safety plans. But even in this short time you may be able to get a restraining order that prohibits the abuser from having any contact with you.

Do restraining orders work? As many women have discovered, restraining orders aren't always effective. Nevertheless, they make it easier to get further help if that's necessary. Sometimes the police will maintain a protective surveillance. After the initial order, a permanent restraining order will require that you appear again before a judge. In many communities, a volunteer victim advocate is at the courthouse, ready to help you with paperwork and to appear in court with you. A court appearance will be easier if someone accompanies you—perhaps a pastor, a church leader or a trusted friend.

FOR SPIRITUAL REFLECTION

Seven corpses hanging from a gibbet were silhouetted against the darkening sky. The fading light fell on the figure of a weary, emaciated woman. Slumped on a rock, she kept watch over the decomposing bodies. A slight rustle caused the woman to start up suddenly and to hurl a well-aimed stone at a shadow skulking toward one of the corpses.

Rizpah was guarding the remains of her two sons and five stepgrandsons day and night. As a concubine of the fallen King Saul, she had known his irrational rages and his murderous tendencies. David had managed to escape, but others had not been so blessed. The maddened king had attempted a genocide against the Gibeonites. Long before, Joshua had been tricked into promising their forefathers safe haven in the land of Israel (Joshua 9:15, 18-26). No matter that the Gibeonites had practiced deception, God's people must still keep their promise and allow them to remain as aliens in the land. Saul's massacre was a violation of trust and of a covenant before God. When David, the new king, consulted God as to the cause of a three-year drought, he was told that it lay in Saul's violent and sacrilegious action. Expiation must be made.

Although the remaining Gibeonites were a minority with few legitimate rights, they met David's request for their blessing with an insistence that seven of Saul's offspring (perhaps ringleaders in the atrocity) must be delivered to them for execution. They understood well the principle of retaliation that characterized much of Israel's law. David offered them a payment of money, but they refused (2 Samuel 21:4), for the law declared that the appropriate sentence was not ransom but death (Numbers 35:30-34). When presented with the opportunity, the disenfranchised clamored for the right of blood vengeance—under the most grisly conditions that they could invent.

As secondary wife of the perpetrator, Rizpah had no right to resist when David handed Saul's sons and grandsons over to the Gibeonites. Only the sons of Jonathan were spared. The Gibeonites executed the seven quickly and left them unburied on a hill in Gibeon. According to

Deuteronomy 21:22-23, bodies of those punished by hanging must be buried by nightfall. But the Gibeonites, not being part of the faith community, felt no compulsion to obey this rule.

Proper burial had been denied, but God had not forgotten, nor had Rizpah. Decent burial is a basic human right even of those who die by execution. Just as an abused woman suffers a violation of human rights, so too had Rizpah. There were many in Israel who should have made a protest, but we have no record that anyone did—just as sometimes faith communities today fail to support their members who are abused.

Rizpah remembered all too bitterly how the mutilated body of the slain Saul, along with those of his sons and attendants killed in battle, had been hung up for public display by the Philistines in the public square of Beth-Shan. The desecration had been too much for the citizens of Jabesh-Gilead, who came by night and transported the dead for proper burial in their territory under a tamarisk tree. Then they observed a proper period of mourning (1 Samuel 31:8-13). But for the seven on the hill, there was no such dignified burial.

If she could not protest in words, Rizpah could become a living monument. By day she guarded the bodies against the birds and at night against the beasts. With sticks, stones, clubs, shrieks and curses she drove them off. Day after day and night after night she kept her vigil, snatching brief periods of rest on a piece of sackcloth spread over the rock. During the worst of the heat, the sackcloth became an awning above her head.

Under the searing sun, the flesh peeled away from the whitening bones, while the insects buzzed unceasingly. Then there was the interminable stench, the rotting of bodies that had once been safe within her own womb.

The Bible tells us that Rizpah took up her station at the first of the harvest and continued on throughout the summer, until at last the rains fell. The drought was over, expiation had been made, and she had not failed those dear to her. She had not budged from what she knew to be right, and her very presence spoke what her voice could not. David had an obligation toward her dead that he had not met.

As the falling rain heralded a healing of the drought-stricken land, David was told of Rizpah's fidelity, and her unyielding perseverance stirred his conscience. Previously David had praised the piety of the citizens of Jabesh-Gilead in burying Saul and Jonathan with proper respect (1 Samuel 31:11-13; 2 Samuel 2:5). In his elegy for father and son, he had called on the daughters of Israel to raise their voices in mourning (2 Samuel 1:24), but Rizpah and her sons had escaped his notice. Now he was forced to recognize his own failure. He gathered the bones from the gibbet on Gibeon's hill and retrieved those from Jabesh-Gilead, uniting the family of Saul in death. All were honorably buried as befitted the anointed king of Israel. A voiceless and marginalized woman had prevailed in her search for justice.

🌹

Rowena's[1] husband had broken several of her ribs and run over her foot with an automobile. As the abuse escalated, he had kicked her into unconsciousness. When she recovered, she came to the conclusion that she must escape to save her life. She had been isolated from friends and family and was living on a lonely rural road. She made it to safety by hiding in a henhouse until she could get transportation to a women's shelter.

At first she was so shaken that she could not take advantage of the helpful programs she was offered. As her mind cleared, little by little she was able to make some decisions. The first important decision was that she would give her life to following Jesus Christ. Now she had found the love that never fails, the kindness and grace of God. This was deep nurture to her hungry soul. She was reunited with her family of origin and found as well a new family in Christ.

Her second decision was that a divorce was necessary if her husband was to be prevented from killing her. A relative gave her the name of a lawyer, and shelter workers accompanied her to court in order to protect her. The judge issued a temporary order, and Rowena was given a small amount of financial provision.

Shortly before the next court date, I (Cathie) had just met Rowena, and this time she asked me to accompany her. We sat outside the courtroom on a bench while her husband prowled, pacing in a circle around us. The lawyers disappeared into the chambers and seemed to be gone for a very long time.

When Rowena's lawyer reappeared, he announced that the case had been heard, and Rowena's settlement was a very small share of the family business that she had worked hard to build. Although I was not familiar with the court system of that state, I protested that it was not fair to have reached that decision without allowing Rowena to present her case to the judge. Neither Rowena nor her husband had appeared before him. We were told that the judge did not wish to see her and that the matter was settled.

"But this is not fair," I said, and the lawyer agreed. I began to recall news about corruption in the legal system of this state. An election was soon to be held, and I promised the lawyer that I would do my best to inform women that the judge would not even grant Rowena access to his courtroom. "I understand that this judge is campaigning on a promise to be supportive of women's concerns," I said.

"This is not a woman's concern," the lawyer countered.

"Oh yes, it is," I insisted. "She was an abused wife, and justice needs to be done."

With that the lawyer disappeared again into the courtroom; soon he reemerged to say that at a future date Rowena might plead her case before the judge.

Time passed, and Rowena was given no notification of a court date. She heard of a case in which the same attorney had accepted a bribe. Had he represented her fairly behind those closed doors? There was no way that she could afford to hire another lawyer, and the shelter could offer no option. Ordinarily women would settle just to have custody of their children, but Rowena had no children and was already middle-aged. She needed to have a share of the assets of the business in which she had been an equal partner.

I told her the story of the widow and the unrighteous judge and of how at last she achieved justice (Luke 18:1-8). Jesus told that story and then went on to promise that God will see that those who cry for justice receive it.

Since Rowena had not been allowed into the courtroom, I suggested, what if she sent a registered letter to the judge, explaining the way she had been treated, the worth of the business and her need for a financial settlement? It took awhile for her to collect her thoughts and organize them well, but in time she composed a letter and sent it by registered mail.

A court date was assigned, but she was allowed to take no one with her to the hearing. All her Christian friends promised to pray that she would be treated fairly. Rowena's former lawyer was there, though she had not invited him. The circle of males around her was intimidating. We had told her of Christ's promise that God would give his followers the words to say when they were brought before a magistrate (Matthew 10:19-20). Still, she was beginning to panic.

Her husband's lawyer started the questioning in a hostile mode in order to upset her composure. Flustered and off base, she answered his questions about the financial arrangements as best she could. As he continued to press, she blurted out a truthful response—that her husband had not filed income taxes for a number of years.

Suddenly she was dismissed and awarded an amount far higher than she had dared to hope.

Her explanation was quite simple: "It wasn't me on the witness stand—it was the Holy Spirit!" Like Rizpah, she was rewarded for seeking justice.

HOW DO I GET STARTED
ON THE HEALING JOURNEY?

YOU NEED TO COUNT ON MANY UNEXPECTED BENDS in the road as you journey toward healing and wholeness. Sometimes it will seem the pathway is leading you nowhere. Sometimes you will feel overwhelmed by the number of obstacles or the steepness of the slope. Yet there will be other moments when you will be surprised to find how far you have come in just a short time. The healing journey is like that.

Finding the place you are looking for—longing for—can prove far more complicated than you might first have thought. Or maybe it will be a bit easier than some ill-informed but well-meaning friends have suggested. When you finally reach a hoped-for destination, you can be let down or even bitterly disappointed by the place you have chosen to go or the people with whom you have sought refuge.

Before you make any important change in your life, you need to know that some days things will look bleak, the sun will not shine, you will be engulfed in thick fog or torrents of rain. Your knee-jerk reaction will be to give up. But knowing ahead of time that the journey is like that will help you have strength in the midst of obstacles, stick to it when people you trust let you down, and maintain realistic expectations of yourself, of friends and family members, of your church and its leaders, and of professional staff in community agencies.

Others can help you, offer you direction or guidance, support you when your body and your emotions are especially vulnerable. But ultimately, you embark on the healing journey by yourself. It is your journey and yours alone. For the Christian believer, however, there is One who walks alongside no matter how steep or treacherous the path. *The promise is clear: you will never walk alone!*

YOU NEVER KNOW

I had some trouble finding the church in the early morning hours before the workshop began. Its denomination was "mainstream," but its location was not. Isolated in a seedy neighborhood of an industrial city, the building looked rundown—and as I learned later, so did the minister.

I had been asked to lead a workshop for pastoral training, discussing issues related to disclosure of abuse, making referrals and following up. But at ten minutes before time to begin, no one had shown up, except the church secretary. She informed me that she was not a *volunteer*—as if being a volunteer was something to be ashamed of. On the contrary, she was a member of the *paid* staff.

What an unwelcoming place, I thought to myself. *This isn't at all what I expected. Maybe I should get out of here as fast as possible.* The middle-aged woman led me to the basement; I followed, struggling with several boxes of materials, as she marched ahead empty-handed.

Downstairs I noticed that the stench of unclean toilets was strong in the air. "From bad to worse," I muttered under my breath.

"You can set up the tables and chairs for about seventy-five," the secretary informed me.

"Okay," I heard my voice reply. She left and I began to look for extra chairs and tables in the surrounding classrooms. Eventually I found an overhead projector, dusty from months of sitting without use. Before long I had worked up a sweat. But for what purpose? It was now nine o'clock and no one had come.

About ten minutes later the ministers began arriving. First came the host pastor, a rather unkempt, angry man. He obviously resented the fact that his superiors had organized a district event in *his* church, so his response had been to misinform me of its start time. Several times throughout the day, he tried to derail the discussion and the focus of our meeting. But his attempts were unsuccessful, not because I cleverly outwitted him but because the other pastors in attendance really cared about the topic and created a warm, interested learning environment.

Still, for me the day was quite a trial. I was being directly challenged by the host minister at every turn. I didn't know what his agenda was or why he was putting up obstacles. The discussion part of the workshop was like a tennis match: the audience watched as the ball bounced into my court, then into his.

But as I was gathering my materials, preparing to go home, a young pastor approached me, holding out his hand to shake mine. As he spoke words of appreciation, his hand held mine tightly, refusing to let go. Then tears filled his eyes: "I was a child victim of abuse. I know exactly what you are talking about, for I lived it for many years. The resistance of [the host pastor] helped us all to see even more clearly the importance of your message, the reality of abuse and the long, long journey toward wholeness."

His tight grip said eloquently, *Each of us needs to face our own reality, chart our own travels, no matter how difficult a process that may be, or how long it will take to get where we are trying to go.*

A setting may be unpleasant and unwelcoming, our efforts can appear to be failing. Yet as we pursue the truth, the results are transformative. Personal growth can happen when we least expect it.

Again, the journey will be difficult. There are many hard truths to face in our own lives and in the lives of others. Facing reality can be very painful. Facing reality can make us angry or deeply depressed. Sometimes people want to prevent others from facing reality. They prefer to close their eyes and pretend that the hurt and the shame will simply disappear.

For a victim of abuse there is no easy way to face reality, for there are several hurdles to overcome. Of course battered women differ from one another, in personality and in circumstances. That means that hurdles that are very difficult for some are less challenging for others. But as each hurdle is overcome, the result will be life-changing. Getting started is as easy, or as difficult, as facing the first hurdle.

HURDLE 1: THE LIE OF WORTHLESSNESS

Claire[1] is a middle-aged single woman who serves as a Salvation Army officer in an urban area. Her work focuses on the poor. In the neighborhoods where she ministers, many streets are unsafe at night. Claire knows only too well of the vulnerability facing women on their own.

Over the years of her ministry, Claire has witnessed many things. She has been called to assist in countless situations of abuse. In the crisis, many women victims wondered whether it was finally time to leave their home, temporarily or forever. Claire reflected on the similarities of their lives: a very controlling man, beatings in a fit of rage, remorse. Betty was just one example.

Betty arrived at the Salvation Army shelter one night after Jack had assaulted her. Betty needed housing, food and protection. There were spiritual concerns as well. Over the following weeks, sometimes Betty blamed God for her troubles, believing that it was God's fault that she was "in this mess."

Claire struggled to share the hope of the gospel and the love of God with Betty. Although Claire assured her, "God loves you for who you are," Betty didn't believe her. And why would she? It was far too difficult to believe that God could love her when she didn't even like herself. It was far too difficult to see God as caring for her when the person on earth she loved deeply treated her so badly. Still, while Betty found it hard to accept Claire's words, she was quick to accept the practical support

Claire offered, such as financial assistance, clothing and food.

Betty moved back home once it seemed Jack was mending his ways. But eventually he attacked her again, and again she had to leave. This pattern repeated itself four or five times. The repeated moves were extremely hard on Betty, but they were very difficult for Claire too. As her pastor, she wondered how Betty could so easily go back to the man who hurt her body and wounded her heart. Although Claire wanted the church's door to be always open to Betty, the repetitive pattern of her escape and return began to look like a losing battle.

Claire talked to Betty about how a woman's level of self-esteem affects whether or not she will seek help and whether or not she will escape from a home that threatens to destroy her. The options she presented to Betty often fell on unreceptive ears. Because Jack had told her for so long that she was "no good," Betty actually believed she was of little value. In Claire's words, "she believed the garbage he told her." Believing the lie kept Betty from seeking to change the circumstances of her life.

When Betty is able—perhaps with the help of someone else who can be trusted—to question what Jack has told her about her value as a person, she may be ready to start the healing journey.

One of the first hurdles for an abused woman is the lies. But letting go of lies is much easier to say than to do.

You may have been told for a very long time that you are stupid, ugly or useless. *It is a lie.* Stop believing it. You have the power to jump the first hurdle.

Like Betty, you may have been told by your abuser that you are worthless. You may have believed the lie, or maybe you still believe it. As a result, you may feel useless, worthless or of little value. Facing reality will mean moving from a distorted view of who you are to an accurate assessment of your value and worth.

When you have stopped believing the lies told to you by your abuser, the first hurdle is behind you. Later on in your journey, as you reflect on the past, you will find it remarkable that the lies impacted you so deeply and for so long. Once you see the lies for what they are, part of the deceptive plan of the abuser to keep you from realizing your full potential as a person, they will have much less power over you. This should be good news, even if you are not there yet.

Hurdle 2: Fear That the Future Could Be Worse Than the Past

Facing reality is hard work. It is especially difficult for an abused women who has very few marketable skills and very limited education. She may also have few close friends and lack support from her extended family. Then what do you have? A woman who is very afraid that if she moves on in her life and out of the abusive home, her health, her condition or her fate might get even worse.

Edith, age fifty, is receiving help through some Salvation Army outreach programs. Edith is very worried about her oldest child, Catriona,[2] who lives in a common-law relationship and suffers physical and sexual violence. Edith tells of beatings, a rape, the loss of money. Recently her daughter's partner took whatever money he could find in the apartment and left her with a broken nose. This is just the latest in a string of violations that have occurred during their relationship.

Mona, an officer with the Army, listens intently to Edith's story—it is all too familiar. Mona mentions some of the community resources available to help Catriona, but Edith just shakes her head. Catriona is too frightened to go to the police. Besides, this boyfriend is the best she has ever had; others were much worse. Edith explains that Catriona has had a series of demeaning and damaging relationships with men.

Though she expresses her worries to Mona, Edith doesn't really give much support to her daughter. Edith's own life has been rough, and the challenges facing her are great. There is little that she can offer to someone else, even her own flesh and blood.

In a situation like this, referring somebody to a community program doesn't work very well. "We work with people with their hurts and their bruises and their broken bones as they come to us for food or to join a program or to be in a support group," Mona explains. There are simply too many needs and too few helpers. And finding other sources of community help is not really of much interest to many people the Salvation Army serves. Many of them are very vulnerable women, with little family contact, who feel rejected by just about everybody. They have very little trust left.

A downward spiral into the depths of despair can seem almost inevitable for women caught in a web of persistent unhappiness, low self-esteem, little income, and ongoing verbal, physical and sexual abuse. In Catriona's case, her mother wants to help but is unable. So Edith contacts the Salvation Army, the organization that has helped her in various ways through the years. Despite Mona's faith and the resources of the Salvation Army, she can't do much to help Catriona until the abused woman faces her fear of a future without her current (abusive) partner. For different reasons, neither Mona nor Edith is able to provide a way of escape until Catriona is ready to begin a new life free from the abuse of the past. In order to do that, she must believe in the promise of a better tomorrow.

Some of your own family members may have been unhelpful or unsupportive in the midst of your despair. Like Catriona, you may have suffered in more than one relationship. Hopelessness may permeate your life so deeply that it is impossible to believe that tomorrow could be better than today. Seeking help from a number of agencies seems to require too much courage and too much self-confidence. Because you feel so bad about yourself, you are reluctant to ask anyone for assistance.

When you can begin to imagine that the future *could* be brighter than the past, you are well on your way to overcoming the second hurdle. Many abused women tell stories of coming to their senses. Like the prodigal son, one day they simply see that with a plan in place, tomorrow could bring new possibilities (see Luke 15:14-20). The road will still be long, there are many more hurdles and other rocky patches, but once a destination free of violence is in sight, the next step becomes possible.

HURDLE 3: THE DIFFICULTY OF TAKING ACTION

It is very hard for victims to talk about their abuse, and as you know only too well, it is even harder to take the first step toward looking for help. In other words, there is a wide gap between insight and action.

Earlier in the book, in chapter two, we discussed various ways that women begin to reveal to others that there is violence in their lives. Sometimes they focus on other problems; sometimes they disclose part of the story; and sometimes they have the strength to say right out loud, "I am being abused." Just as there are a variety of ways to name what is happening in your life, so there are many ways to look for help, as the following story reveals.

Margaret has been serving as an officer in the Salvation Army for many years, doing inner-city ministry in various regions of the country. As a pastoral counselor, she finds that the men and women who seek her help often talk first about their money problems.

She told the story of Karen,[3] a military wife; like Margaret, she had been uprooted numerous times when the army needed her husband to move. Karen and John had several children. Despite her desperate efforts, Karen was unable to make the portion of John's paycheck she was given for housekeeping stretch far enough to pay for food for the family and clothing of the children. John was very controlling of the family finances and expected her to make do with an allowance that was totally unreasonable. If she ran short, as was often the case, he simply retorted that she had been given money and if it was all gone, tough luck—he was not giving her any more.

Karen first sought Margaret's help for budgeting. "What can I do to get things for my children and get groceries too?" In the safety of her small church office, Margaret learned that Karen's last resort was to go to the food bank. She was ashamed to seek this help, but there was little else she could do. Karen was very, very fearful of what would happen if John found out she was getting groceries in this manner. But often he wasn't home, sometimes for extended periods, when his military duties would take him far away. So it was unlikely that he would find out about her trips to the food bank.

The Salvation Army officer tried to piece together the complicated web of interactions in John and Karen's family life. Maybe John didn't realize how bad the problems were or how much despair Karen felt. Maybe, since he was away so much, he didn't have an opportunity to see for himself that the kids needed shoes. Maybe it was hard for him to understand that children's feet do grow. There were so many "maybes."

In this family there was a lot of verbal abuse—screaming, yelling and name-calling. While Margaret suspected that at times John became physically violent, it was his controlling behavior that had brought Karen to call for help.

Unfortunately, by the time the relationship between Margaret and Karen had become secure, Margaret was called on to move to a new Salvation Army assignment.

Like Karen, you may be called names and verbally abused. These are forms of controlling behavior. This may come with physical abuse, but it may not. Like Karen, you may have begun your search for help by trying to change your own behavior. You may (or may not) be hoping that sensitive friends and caregivers will look beyond the initial reasons you gave for seeking help. It may have taken a lot of courage to tell your story to someone else and then consider what options you have for change.

In telling our stories, whether we are abuse victims or not, we weave who we are and how we feel into a larger life story, a way of understanding ourselves. Telling our stories helps us all to gain insight into what choices are ours to make, what options are before us. In telling our stories, our pain may be affirmed. In these ways we gain the strength to rock the boat, to move from thinking or talking to action. As you overcome this hurdle, you will be ready to plan your next steps.

HURDLE 4: RELUCTANCE TO FIGURE OUT WHAT'S WRONG

At the beginning of the book, we said that a relationship is not healthy when you are belittled, called names, threatened, hurt, isolated, monitored, disrespected, ignored, embarrassed or blamed for all family problems. The stories of Mildred and Brenda in chapter one show clearly that an abuse victim can be young or old, with or without advanced education, in or out of poverty, married or common-law, caring for elderly relatives or awaiting the birth of a first child. Despite their very differing circumstances, Mildred and Brenda were both very frightened women, and their narratives reveal that abuse can happen to anyone at any stage along the life course.

What does differ among women is whether or not you are able to break the silence surrounding your abuse. For many battered wives, this means you must stop believing lies you've been told, start believing that the future can be brighter than the past, and rock the boat by taking action. Often that action begins with an assessment of what is wrong in your life and in your home.

When there is abuse, assessing risk is very important. Yet it can be a difficult task. Pastors and others in ministry are sometimes uncomfortable asking questions. As an abused woman, you may be uncomfortable giving too many specifics about your circumstances. Maybe you even deny the level of risk to yourself—and there's no doubt that your abuser also denies or minimizes what is happening. One abuser said to his pastor that he didn't think there was any problem with him. "Most of the problems were with the wife, and if she would simply do what he said, then everything would be well." The pastor noted that the wife had good reason to fear her husband, for he had threatened to kill her.[4]

What can one do in these circumstances? It is very important to listen to the clues dropped throughout a conversation. Being a good listener, being sensitive to what is really being said, can save a life. A very good listener will be able to pick up on the clues that you as a victim are intending to drop in a conversation and perhaps even clues you haven't intended. A good listener will ask questions and dig a little deeper to sort out the hints.

Assessing What Is Wrong

Here are some of the ways pastors have assessed that something dreadful is happening in the life of a woman seeking their help.[5] Ask yourself whether any of these things are occurring in your life.

You know something is dreadfully wrong when . . .

Food intake is controlled.	She was given an allowance. . . . There was a lock on the fridge door.
Freedom is limited.	He made all the decisions. . . . He wouldn't even allow her to grocery shop.
There is torture.	He's the aggressor . . . and there was an intentional holding of her head under water. . . . She must completely submit to him.
There is intimidation.	He needs total control through physical power. . . . Shotguns were involved.
There are no joint decisions.	Everything revolves around him. . . . She's in fear.
The human spirit is dying.	He sexually assaulted her a number of times, but he never, ever threatened to kill her, but she was slowly dying.
There is emotional abandonment.	He had already left her twenty-four months earlier psychologically.
There is physical abuse.	She has been thrown literally against the wall. And after throwing her against the wall, he disappears and doesn't come home sometimes overnight, or for a day or so.
Safety is a concern.	Her personal safety was in jeopardy.

Assessing risk for yourself and for your children is very, very important. You may need an outsider—a trusted friend, a pastor or a therapist—to help you see just how much risk there is to your mental and physical health. If you live in fear, then you are not safe. If you walk on eggshells, there is a problem that shouldn't be ignored any longer. Don't forget about risks to your children; they have no power in the situation. If your emotional health can't be guaranteed and if you think your children are in danger, it's time to seek outside input. It's time to say, "We need help." Safety must be your first priority—your safety and that of your children.

HURDLE 5: THE STRUGGLE TO FIGURE OUT WHAT HELP YOU NEED

Once you have realized that your safety cannot be guaranteed in your home, it's time to develop a safety plan that will allow you to escape the next time there is danger. But figuring out what help is needed is not as straightforward as it may seem. It's actually one of the hurdles you have to face. As with other hurdles, depending on the circumstances of your life and your knowledge of community resources, this may be a greater or lesser hurdle for you.

Do you have permanent employment? Are there children in the home? Do you have any independent resources—money in a separate account, your own car, investments? Are there family members who will help if you ask? Do you need to see a lawyer? Do you have transportation? Will a restraining order be required?

Often there are physical needs, emotional needs, financial needs and spiritual needs. Thinking through all of your immediate and longer-term requirements can seem rather overwhelming, especially since you have no doubt lived through years of being told that you can't do anything right.

An initial conversation with a pastor or a shelter staff member will help you find out what resources are available in your community and how you might make use of them. These most often include legal help,

Figuring Out What Help You Need

Here are some of the ways hundreds of pastors have tried to serve abused women.[6] Some of these "intervention strategies" may be very helpful for you. It is up to you to *ask for help*. And if the first person you ask is unable or unwilling to offer assistance, *ask someone else*.

THE NEED	THE WORDS OF ONE WHO HELPED
Do you need rescue for yourself and/or the children?	She was rescued and so were the children . . .
Do you need someone to come and respond to the abuser?	. . . And when the perpetrator was a danger to himself as well as to others, I was a bit of an escape hatch for him, or kept him alive.
Do you need someone who is a good listener?	I don't pretend to be a professional. . . . I have a deep desire to be a sounding board to those who need it.
Do you need a strong shoulder to cry on?	We had chatted and she just fell apart in my arms. And it almost felt like the whole weight of the whole stress level was right here on your shoulder blade. . . . She had been so stoic for so long.
Do you need to hear words that condemn the abuse you have suffered?	She did not deserve to get hit.
Do you need to have your self-esteem built up, or do you need to develop certain skills?	Listen and help her with her self-esteem. Encourage her first of all, to learn to drive . . . to refuse to be the doormat in the community . . . to start putting a value on her work . . . get some training.
Do you need spiritual counsel?	I was able to give her somebody that she could unload on. . . . I was able to help her understand that she was not to blame herself.
Do you need spiritual support?	I really feel that spiritually you stand with the victim. I guess sometimes I just feel like I have to hold their spirits while they're doing the work.
Do you need suggestions about assistance that is available (referral sources)?	I saw the bruise. . . . I saw her for about three months and I realized that there was a lot more depth. . . . It was escalating, so I told her I would never let her down but I did think we needed to look at more skilled intervention.

medical assistance, police, psychological or psychiatric support, school-based services, financial help from state social services, job training, temporary shelter at a transition house and self-help groups. How to explore the forms of help available was discussed more fully in the last chapter, but it is important to point out again that you need to be in charge of your own healing journey. No one else, no matter how good their intentions are, can decide exactly what you need. And no one can figure out the right schedule for your healing process. What others *can* do, depending on their skills and willingness to be involved, is to respond to specific needs once you have called on them for help.

Simply facing reality is a very difficult process for any battered Christian woman—because your reality is not simple or easy. You have to overcome several hurdles. There are both practical and spiritual needs. And often there is great fear.

Maybe you feel great fear right at this moment, as you read. But looking carefully at the risks in your life and figuring out what sources of assistance are available in your church and community will enable you to face your own reality, as grim as it may seem. Facing reality can be the first step on the road to healing and wholeness. Every journey begins with a first step!

FOR SPIRITUAL REFLECTION

It is exceedingly difficult for an abused woman to maintain a clear perspective. Often her abuser has told her that she is stupid, fat, ugly, incompetent and unable to take care of herself. All too often she believes this, because she has heard it so often. She becomes less and less able to help herself, able to think clearly, able to make plans to make sure that the abuse stops.

The problem may be made worse when the woman seeks help from her pastor, an elder or deacon, or a friend in the church. If she is told that she's to blame and she has to become a better wife, or if she is told simply to live with the situation, her outlook is likely to become still more distorted. And she and her children are at even greater risk.

The Bible tells a wonderful story of a woman who kept her perspective when the lives of her children were at risk. Abigail was married to a man whose very name meant "churl" or "fool." The Hebrew word *nabal* implies lack of good judgment in thought, word, deed and attitude. Proverbs is talking about people like Nabal when it says, "If the wise go to law with fools, there is ranting and ridicule without relief. . . . A fool gives full vent to anger, but the wise quietly holds it back" (Proverbs 29:9, 11). "The fool throws off restraint and is careless. One who is quick-tempered acts foolishly" (Proverbs 14:16-17).

"Now the name of the man was Nabal, and the name of his wife Abigail. The woman was clever and beautiful, but the man was surly and mean" (1 Samuel 25:3). Apparently his bad behavior had earned him his name, for Abigail later said to King David, "My lord, do not take seriously this ill-natured fellow, Nabal; for as his name is, so is he; Nabal is his name, and folly is with him" (1 Samuel 25:25). Certainly no one was in a better position to know this than his wife.

A man like this had surely not treated Abigail with kindness and respect, but she had been able to maintain balance in her understanding of his dealings. Although Nabal was rich, he, like other Israelites living in the wilderness, needed protection for his flocks. David, who was also living in the wilderness to stay far from the murderous King Saul, put his fellow refugees to work. David's men patrolled the sparsely populated land and drove off bandits who would have stolen the livestock. In return, the owners gave payment to David's posse.

But when Nabal was approached, he refused to send any payment for the protection that had been given. Nabal's rejection was both snide and arrogant. Why should he take some of the good food he had set aside for his own workmen and send it off to David? Who was David anyway? A person of questionable parentage.

To insult someone's mother is always dangerous!

While the messengers took off to tell David what the sneering Nabal had said, Nabal's own staff brought the news to Abigail. She immediately understood the danger to the entire household and took action to repair the damage. While David started down the mountain with a war party of four hundred men ready to exterminate Nabal and all his house, Abigail started up the mountain with her staff. In her caravan were mules loaded with all kinds of foods: two hundred loaves of bread, two skins of wine, five butchered sheep, five measures of parched grain, a hundred clusters of raisins and two hundred cakes of figs.

She understood only too well the danger into which her husband's poor judgment had plunged the whole family. Many an abused woman is paralyzed in such situations, but not Abigail. In this matter of life and death, her action was swift, decisive and highly diplomatic. Instead of denying her husband's wrongdoing or excusing him, she told David frankly that Nabal had been wrong and that she had come to make amends. She actually took responsibility and assumed the leadership for keeping her family safe. Her level-headed response would not only save the lives of the family but also restrain the hot-headed David from committing a very serious crime.

Many women cannot see beyond their immediate and overwhelming crisis, but Abigail could consider the long-range implications. Her wisdom was gained through spiritual contemplation, looking at the righteousness and purposes of God. With the insight of a prophet, she declared to David:

> The LORD will certainly make my lord a sure house, because my lord is fighting the battles of the LORD; and evil shall not be found in you so long as you live. . . . When the LORD has done to my lord according to all the good that he has spoken concerning you, and has appointed you prince over Israel, my lord shall have no cause of grief, or pangs of conscience, for having shed blood without cause or for having saved himself. (1 Samuel 25:28-31)

David responded with gladness: "Blessed be the LORD, the God of Is-rael, . . . and blessed be you, who have kept me today from bloodguilt and from avenging myself by my own hand! For as surely as the LORD the God of Israel lives, . . . unless you had hurried and come to meet me, truly by morning there had not been left to Nabal so much as one male" (1 Samuel 25:33-34).

It is important for women to maintain a realistic view of what is hap-pening in their life. There can be terrible consequences when a woman reproaches herself, feels that she is to blame, and accepts the abuser's evaluation of her as stupid, incompetent, crazy or unbalanced. All of this makes it impossible for her to find a positive solution. And it's not safe to assume that she must simply accept abuse as the will of God for her life. The first step is to understand, like Abigail, that the situation is dan-gerous and contrary to the will of God. Then something must be done about it.

Robert,[7] an avid Bible reader with a history of mental illness, was ter-rorizing his wife and children. He constantly insisted that they "submit to him in everything" and as a result reduced the entire household to ut-ter misery. In desperation his wife, Matilda, consulted a therapist. The psychologist heard her story and said, "I think I can help you—on one condition. I think your problems have a lot to do with your religion. I will work with you as long as you are willing to consider some other re-sponse than submission."

Matilda simply walked out of his office. Above all things, she wanted to do the will of God, no matter what the price. Her husband had cer-tainly taught her that submission was God's will for wives, and she would not go against the Bible. She went home and tried even harder to be submissive, but things only got worse.

At last she found a Christian therapist, who agreed to see both her and Robert separately. After a few sessions the therapist asked, "Why do you allow your thinking to be distorted by your husband's illness?"

That question was a shock to Matilda. She did know that the abuse was taking a terrible toll on her children. Was she supposed to let her husband do all the thinking for the family? Were the Scriptures saying something that she had been missing?

She had read Geoffrey Chaucer's medieval tale of patient Griselda and how her patience had eventually turned her husband sweet. Somehow Matilda had made Griselda her mental model of a godly wife. But was this really *God's* pattern? Matilda now began to study the biblical story of Abigail, who acted independently of her husband in order to save her children. Did she too have the responsibility for right action to preserve her family?

Other Scriptures began to lead her to an answer to this question. Matilda's role as helpless victim appeared less and less appropriate. God had called her to be a woman of strength, and her cowering attitude had only encouraged her husband's sinful conduct.

As her attitude began to change, based on biblical convictions, Robert's behavior began to change too. The stronger Matilda grew in her understanding of the Word of God, the more balanced her husband became. Although the road was rocky at times, her gentle but firm insistence on new patterns of relationship brought peace within the household.

WHAT STEPS DO I TAKE
TO GET ON WITH MY LIFE?

EVERY JOURNEY BEGINS WITH A FIRST STEP. When the path is rough and the slope steep, as it is on your healing journey, there are many hurdles to jump and obstacles to overcome. We have tried to outline some of the challenges you will be facing. But remember that every woman's journey is a little different. And the path you are following will not always seem straight. Sometimes you'll feel you are going in circles or making sharp turns as you wind your way up the mountain of recovery. Other times there will be roadblocks.

In this chapter, we focus on the key steps you will need to take as you get on with your life after you have broken the silence about your abuse and sought help from your church and within your community.

STEP ONE: DARE TO DREAM

Last year I visited Croatia—a nation of people who have experienced much violence, despair and struggle. As I traveled within this eastern European country, I noticed how much effort was required for daily living. In the faces of old men and women and in the voices of the young, I saw and heard discouragement and little hope.

The orphanages were especially hopeless: so many children, so little space, so few workers. Despite the noble intentions of those who were caring for children not their own, the future prospects of girls and boys living in the orphanages were not bright. Many would end up on the streets. Some of the girls would grow up, get pregnant, and bring their own babies to an orphanage, and the cycle would be repeated.

Yet in the midst of what might be regarded as great despair, there was a bright light. Gentle Breezes[1] was a transition home run by a Croatian Christian. Girls who were too old to live any longer in an orphanage could go to Gentle Breezes for a few months to learn life skills, work with others in a small business and then graduate to independent living. When I visited Gentle Breezes for the first time, the young residents prepared afternoon tea, a new skill they had just learned. On my second visit, some months later, I was able to have a long conversation with one of the young women living there.

Sonja[2] told me that life in the orphanage was predictable; everyone was treated the same. There was food, a bed, clothes and occasional activities. The discipline was harsh, the routine boring.

"Did you ever try to run away?" I asked.

A perplexed look crossed her face. "Where would I run to?" came the reply.

"Were you ever afraid?"

Her only fear was that at some point she would have to leave the sheltered environment of the orphanage and begin life on her own, without money, without skills.

Then we spoke of Sonja's new life in Gentle Breezes. Here five young women, with a couple of trained workers, were learning to tend a garden, prepare meals, clean house and create beautiful candles for sale. Sonja grinned when I asked how life was different now. "In every way," came the reply.

As our conversation was winding down, I asked one last question. "What were some of your dreams or wishes as a young girl, or as a teen, living with others in an orphanage?"

It took her a long time to answer, and then she replied with words that I will never, ever forget. Sonja whispered: "I didn't dare to dream!"

Daring to dream that tomorrow can be different from today is a key marker of healing, an important step in the journey toward healing and wholeness. On the road to healing, you need to give yourself permission to dream. Tomorrow can be different. With God's power and the support of your church community, daring to dream involves charting your new life free from the abuse of the past. It is a vital step in moving forward. Never forget, walking is just a series of steps. You can only take one step at a time.

STEP TWO: FIND A LISTENING EAR

A second important step in the healing journey is finding someone to talk to, someone to confide in, someone who will listen and affirm the pain you are feeling. To be a "listening ear," quite simply, is to listen intently and quietly to the voice of someone else. You might say that a listening ear is a person whose ears are bigger than their mouth!

It isn't easy to find a person like that. You may try several times before you are successful. But finding the right person is worth the effort. Don't give up if you are let down by the first few people in whom you attempt to confide. Not everyone is gifted at listening and responding with warmth and support. Listening can be hard work. Sometimes it may seem like the Christian community has more tongues than ears!

Barbara and her mother Kathryn live in a rural community on the East Coast, where they attend a Baptist church.[3] When talking to members of Nancy's research team, Barbara lamented her mother's inability to hear her own daughter's story. "She was up here and we were sittin' at the table Saturday night playing a game of Scrabble and she said, 'You know, I just don't understand these transition houses.' She said, 'People lived for years without them, and any woman is a fool that lets a man abuse her!'"

Practical Support and the Healing Journey

What kinds of practical support might I expect from women in my church?

Here are some possibilities, based on interviews by Nancy and her team with 136 evangelical women who had offered support to an abused woman.

Emotional Support

- Listening ear
- Ongoing friendship
- Accompanying me to court hearings
- Sharing her own story of abuse
- Helping with a support group

Physical Support

- Offering temporary shelter—a bed for the night
- Babysitting my children
- Giving me emergency money
- Offering me transportation
- Providing food items
- Loaning or giving me furniture
- Providing indirect financial support

Spiritual Support

- Praying together
- Sharing Scripture verses

Referrals

- Suggesting a transition house
- Suggesting a minister

Advice

- Offering advice as a friend
- Offering advice in a professional context

"And I said, 'Mom, how many times do you think you came to the hospital to see me when my eyes were black and blue, my teeth were driven through my lip, and my throat was cut, that I fell down the stairs or tripped on a sled?'"

It was painful for Barbara to realize that her mother was unable to see clearly what was happening in her life. Kathryn did not have eyes to see or ears to hear the truth of her daughter's life or the pain behind her bruises. For Barbara had married a believer, a church leader no less.

Reflecting on her own journey, Barbara, a middle-aged mother, mused on how many abused women keep the pain locked up their entire life: "They will die with it inside them, because they have nobody that will listen."

For Barbara, as for many other Christian women, the first attempts at finding emotional support fell on deaf ears. It is very disappointing and painful when you reveal the depths of your experience to someone only to find out that they are not really listening.

You need to be prepared: this may happen to you. You may need to give clues to several trusted friends, or more than one church leader, before you find a listening ear.

STEP THREE: ACCEPT HELP

Most of us have a strong streak of independence: we want to *do it by myself*. From the time we were small, we wanted out of the crib, out of the stroller, to walk without holding our mother's hand, to cross the street without an adult, to ride the subway alone—in essence to make our own decisions and find our own way.

In recent months and years you may have been told by your abuser that you couldn't do anything right. Having come to see this as a lie, you now may be very reluctant to place yourself in a situation where you need the help of someone else. This is understandable.

But accepting help from others is not the same thing as being dependent on them. You will need to accept practical support from others as you journey toward full independence. When you have decided what help you need and then are willing to receive it graciously, you will have taken an enormous step forward.

What kind of support you need, of course, depends on your particular circumstances and the gap between what you have and what you require. It also depends on the resources of other women who are willing to fill in that gap. Finally, it is related to what resources are available in your local area.

ONE STEP AT A TIME

Whether you are facing a long climb up a mountain or a leisurely stroll on a sandy beach, the same principle applies: you can only take one step at a time. *Step by step.* When the path is rough and steep and it's hard to get footing, there will be plenty of times that you seem to be taking one step forward and another one back, or sideways. You move forward by inches, winding around obstacles. It is rare that you are able to go straight ahead, onward and upward.

Not all abused women face the same challenges or the same obstacles. The steps in the healing journey will differ depending on the circumstances of your abuse and the skills and talents that make up who you are. Just as you are a unique and much-loved creation of God, so too the steps of your journey will be unique. They will be your steps and yours alone. However, there are some issues that most abused women face. As you read through the steps listed below, pick out those that resemble your travels, what you have faced and what you still need to overcome.

STEPS IN THE HEALING JOURNEY

Here are some of the steps pastors have observed in the healing journey of abused women who have sought help from them.[4]

PROBLEMS ABUSED WOMEN FACE	SOLUTIONS: ACTIVE PARTICIPATION
Being passive, accepting his version of things.	Question the lies.
She had feelings of God abandoning her.	Acknowledge abandonment.
It's choosing the path of least resistance. That's probably her way of contributing to the conflict in the relationship: by staying in an unhealthy relationship.	Begin to rock the boat.
You married this guy and you're supposed to stick it out for better or worse and it's really a hard decision to finally leave. It's one of the hardest decisions I've ever made.	Make hard decisions.
PERPLEXITIES ABUSED WOMEN FACE	**SOLUTIONS: NEW INSIGHTS/ UNDERSTANDINGS**
Because I took those vows in the sight of God, they are sacred vows. How do you break them? And, they are condemned until some minister tells them that if there is no love there, God is not there.	Gain freedom from spiritual condemnation.
The Christian message of resurrection is one of new life. In many cases, this new life will involve recognition that the relationship has died and so divorce becomes the burial.	Resurrection means new life.
I think that she had a spiritual crisis. . . . In the end, the choice was hers to make, and I think that I helped her to be in a better position to be able to make that choice.	Gain freedom to make choices.
He was an elder, well respected within the church and in the community, and he struck her. She had a lot of spiritual questions, like, what's a good Christian wife supposed to do? His life is exactly the way he wants it to be. He had no motivation to change.	The abusive man needs to be challenged.
A lot of people say, "Why don't you talk to them about forgiveness?" . . . But you don't tell a victim to turn around and forgive her abuser when his fist is coming at her. You wait until she is out of it, until she is healed, and then you don't let the anger destroy her inside. And then you talk to her about forgiveness so that she can get on with life. Once the victim becomes a survivor, then it comes time for forgiveness.	The road to forgiveness is long.

THE LONG JOURNEY OF FORGIVENESS

Any discussion of the healing journey eventually comes to the issue of forgiveness.[5] Forgiveness is a complicated theological concept, and it is difficult to do, especially when abuse is what needs to be forgiven. Listen to a discussion among three women in one of our focus groups.

WOMAN 1: I'm almost fifty-one. . . . You can come to a point you think you've forgiven . . . [but] you can't ever forget a severe trauma.

WOMAN 2: We have to forgive in order for us to get healed and get on with it, [but] the forgetting part, you never have confidence in that person again.

WOMAN 3: But I think what, what the apostle Paul meant when he talked about forgetting what is behind, he meant not allowing the past to determine how we live today.[6]

In *Congregational Trauma: Caring, Coping and Learning,* Jill M. Hudson argues that forgiveness is a true theological concept.[7] This means that it is within the body of believers—the church—that we ask the hard questions about forgiveness and learn to accept God's forgiveness of us. "How grateful we should be that God's forgiveness of us is greater than our ability to repent or forgive others."[8]

Over time—and timing is very important in the healing journey—the anger and resentment, the desire for vengeance and punishment, runs its course and can be replaced in the heart of the victim with God's love and God's patience. In this way, forgiveness can be understood as a calling of God to the believer, yet we recognize that both our healing and our capacity to forgive are linked to God's provision of care in our life.[9] When an abused woman is in the midst of the forgiveness process, what a pastor needs most to offer may be a "ministry of presence" rather than a "ministry of words."[10]

Like others who have written about forgiveness, Hudson reminds us of the cry of Jesus from the cross, "Father, forgive them; for they do not know what they are doing" (Luke 23:34). Forgiveness does not erase the pain of the past, nor does it ask us to deny our hurt or pretend it didn't matter. Rather, when forgiveness is complete the pain of the past no longer controls our future path, nor does it trap us in a complicated web of anger and despair.

In *When Good Things Happen to Bad People,* Rabbi Harold Kushner argues that the ability to forgive and the ability to love again are examples of God's empowerment to live in a world that is broken, less than perfect.[11] The community of faith can support the person who feels that in the midst of distress, her faith cannot sustain her. God's faithfulness can be expressed through a faithful church, giving love and care to one who is wounded or betrayed, or who feels that at the moment of trial she is weak. The church may be called to be an intercessor, the link between a woman victim and God.

In *Shattered and Broken,* Rutherford and Linda McDill take issue with the advice that well-intentioned pastors and other church leaders sometimes give to abused women: forgive your husband and return home to be a better wife and mother.[12] They argue that this can put the woman in physical danger and remove her one step further from the help that she desperately needs. "True forgiveness," according to the McDills, "is much more complicated than blind forgiveness."[13]

So what does *true forgiveness* involve? To be sure, it involves the abuser's repentance, not only remorse for the attack but also reflection on what turned his anger into violence, a renunciation of past abusive acts, and a genuine step toward a new way of relating to the woman he once abused.[14]

In her essay "Forgiveness, the Last Step," Marie Fortune argues that forgiveness is a resource available to the pastoral counselor to help women and children who have been abused.[15] It is an important part of the healing process, one means of restoring to wholeness a life that has been shattered by abuse. But forgiveness is the last step in the healing journey, according to Fortune, the last rung on the ladder of the victim's struggle to overcome the brokenness of the past. Forgiveness cannot come before justice or the offender's accountability. Forgiveness that is premature actually damages the healing of both the perpetrator and the victim. Pressure on the victim to quickly "forgive and forget" prevents the abuser from really changing and can be life-threatening for the victim. So it often keeps the abusive cycle going. This is *not* the biblical model of forgiveness taught by Jesus.

True forgiveness can develop after justice has been served. And what are the necessary ingredients of justice?

- truth telling
- recognizing the harm that has been done
- breaking the silence
- listening to the whole story
- refusing to minimize its consequences
- offering protection to the vulnerable—the woman and her dependent children who may still be at risk

Forgiveness responds to justice. It is the process of letting go of both the violent acts themselves and the memories associated with them. Forgiveness is "the choice to no longer allow the memory of the abuse to continue to abuse" one's life.[16] This means that forgiveness "may be the most charitable and compassionate act the church can offer" to victimized women and their children.[17]

Forgiveness is an expression of our relationship with God. At the very least, forgiveness means a victim gives herself permission to look for help and start life afresh. Forgiveness means that you can begin to look at the world without focusing always on the pain of the past. But forgiveness takes a long time, and it doesn't occur in a vacuum. It grows in the soil of acceptance and loving counsel from those who are listening to God's Spirit.

Forgiveness usually has many dimensions:

- acknowledging the wrongdoing
- acknowledging the pain the wrongdoing has caused
- acknowledging who has done terrible wrong
- naming the wrongdoing to others
- grieving the loss of relationship
- grieving the loss of the "happy Christian family" dream
- grieving the breaking of marriage vows
- grieving the lack of support from other family and friends
- grieving the lack of support from some members of the family of faith
- recognizing the anger you feel against the abuser
- recognizing the anger you feel against God
- recognizing the anger you feel against the church or other Christians
- deciding that the past will no longer control the present
- deciding that the future will involve new plans, new ideas
- hungering for a revived spiritual life, born out of crisis
- deciding to focus on some ways that strength has come out of vulnerability or weakness
- seeing yourself as a person who is freed from the damage, anger and resentment of the past

In essence, forgiveness is the believer's response to the healing process in her life. But there are many things that forgiveness is not. It is not easy and does not happen quickly. True forgiveness takes time, lots of time.

Forgiveness *cannot* be

- put on a timetable by someone other than you
- accomplished because somebody else requests or expects it

- offered before you fully understand the pain of the past or its impact
- demanded
- required
- a manipulation of the Christian community to pretend that everything in your family life is OK
- the pastor's reward for his or her hard work
- understood as a guarantee of safety or protection
- understood as a return to things as they were, as if the abuse never happened
- understood to guarantee reconciliation
- a reason for putting yourself or your children in harm's way

And there are several things forgiveness cannot do:

- It cannot precede true repentance.
- It cannot follow a formula.
- It cannot ignore the past.
- It cannot conceal or disguise the anger and pain you feel.
- It cannot occur in isolation of other social or cultural factors.
- It cannot be seen as the same for everyone.

For you as a believer, forgiveness involves the work and assistance of the Holy Spirit. It is part of God's invitation to holy living; in fact, it's a response to a call by God that we all repeat in the words of the Lord's Prayer. Forgiveness reminds us that we ourselves have been forgiven. Forgiveness opens the prayer door of heaven.

As important a process as forgiveness is, it cannot be demanded by the Christian community or a well-intentioned pastor. Just as producing lovely fruit in a garden involves dirty work at the beginning (fertilizing, planting, weeding), so too the promise and possibility of forgiveness grow as you acknowledge your pain, switch your energy from denying to taking action, and become a survivor rather than just a victim.

FOR SPIRITUAL REFLECTION

Tears blinded the eyes of Joseph, and his stomach heaved with the camel's lurching movement across the desert. Sick from the motion and from shock, he could barely comprehend what had happened. The ropes that bound him dug into his arms and legs, confirming that he was really a slave. Between the waves of illness and rage, he fumbled for answers. How could he, the favorite son of his father, be a slave in the hands of greedy traders? How could his brothers have sold him into bondage?

He had seen the silver coins they had been paid for him. How could they betray their own brother in this way? What might they do to his little brother Benjamin now? He had always tried to serve God; how could such terrible things have happened to him, so suddenly?

Joseph was a brilliant young boy, a fact that had not escaped the rest of his family. Brilliance is not easy to live with. He was also good looking and clearly the favorite of his doting father. Special gifts—such as an elegant coat with long sleeves—and preferential treatment had aroused the resentment of Joseph's ten older brothers. Besides that, Joseph tattled on them to their father.[18]

Along with his other gifts, the boy had a remarkable ability to understand dreams and interpret them. Perhaps as a result of observing his siblings' inadequacies, he dreamed that they were in a field binding sheaves of grain. When his sheaf stood upright, those of his brothers bowed down to his. It would have been best to keep such a dream to himself, but the youngster broadcast his vision to the entire family. He then boasted of an even more startling dream. Sun and moon and eleven stars had bowed down to him. Such arrogance offended the entire family and drew a rebuke from his father. "Shall your mother and I and eleven brothers bow to you?"

The brothers were sick of Joseph's superiority. When their father sent him to check on the brothers' shepherding work, they recognized his special coat while he was still in the distance. Suddenly they had a chance to get rid of the brat once and for all. Their first thought was to kill him, but Reuben, the oldest, persuaded them instead to drop him in a pit and leave him there. Later he intended to rescue Joseph and bring him back.

While Reuben was away, though, a caravan of merchants approached, and another brother, Judah, got an idea: Joseph could be sold! The others readily agreed. Twenty pieces of silver were welcome to a family whose wealth was in its livestock. Good riddance to Joseph! They stained the coat with an animal's blood to convince their father that Joseph had been killed in a wild beast's attack. Although Reuben was not involved in the sale of his brother, when he found out what had happened he didn't bother to tell old Jacob the truth.

For Joseph, that camel ride into Egypt meant the end of everything he had known—his identity as his father's beloved, his place as favored member of the family, his belief that one day he would rule his brothers, his confidence in the potential of his gifts and talents. All was lost and up for sale in the slave market of Egypt.

In Egypt Joseph, who had always lived in a tent, saw buildings of stone and brick, decorations of gold and ivory and ebony, a sophisticated culture that was at first bewildering. He was purchased by the captain of Pharaoh's guard, a man used to figuring out what other men could do. He soon assigned the young Hebrew to the position of manager and was delighted with Joseph's ready grasp of administrative tasks. All was entrusted to Joseph, and all was faithfully managed. The Septuagint version of Genesis declares that God poured out his mercy on the young man.

But again Joseph's intelligence and good looks created problems. This time it was sexual harassment. Potiphar's wife invited him to her bed, but Joseph protested that he could not so violate the trust of his master. "How then could I do this great wickedness, and sin against God?" (Genesis 39:9). The woman, humiliated, falsely accused Joseph to her husband, who cast him into the royal prison.

This cruelly unjust imprisonment had been brought about by his own loyalty, and bitterness overwhelmed him. As year followed year in that prison, he had plenty of time to try to make sense of the Bible's most obvious case of domestic abuse. First he had been the victim of his brothers, and then of his master's wife. The King James Version declares, "The iron entered into his soul," but the literal Hebrew is "his soul entered into the iron" (see Psalm 105:18). How well victims of abuse can understand this statement!

The prison director recognized not only Joseph's management skills but also his integrity, and so the prisoner soon became the manager of the prison. All was handled faithfully and well, and Joseph became familiar with Egypt's governmental system. When the chief butler and baker of Pharaoh were thrown into the prison, Joseph had the opportunity to talk with the highest level of court officials. He was able to interpret their dreams and to predict for the butler his restoration to royal favor. Joseph asked only that the butler tell Pharaoh of his own predica-ment and his innocence. But for two years the butler forgot.

When Pharaoh was troubled with a dream that no one could interpret, however, the butler suggested telling it to the Hebrew who claimed that his understanding came from God. Joseph explained Pharaoh's dream as a prediction of seven years of abundance to be followed by seven years of famine. As a result, he was made prime minister of Egypt and was entrusted with managing food production and distribution. It was an administrative position as high as he could have desired—but why was it not with his own people? Why couldn't he use his talents in the way he had foreseen so long ago?

The seven years of plenty passed, and the famine began. By the second year, the family of Jacob was desperate for food, and ten brothers were sent off to buy grain in Egypt. They could not recognize their long-lost brother in the magnificent Egyptian viceroy in charge of the sales, but Joseph saw who they were immediately.

Fighting to control himself and to come up with a strategy for dealing with them, he demanded to know where they had come from. When they said they were from Canaan, he knew beyond a shadow of a doubt that this *was* his own family. He was flooded with emotions: tenderness and bitterness, nostalgia and fury, love and hatred. Each face turned toward him raised childhood memories, sorrows, resentments. And before their faces floated a vision of the sheaves and the stars in his long-ago dreams.

For many years he had waited for this moment, but somehow he had not expected all that he was now feeling. Taking a defensive approach, he accused them of being spies sent to assess Egypt's weak points. The brothers vehemently denied this, insisting that they had come to buy food for their family. As Joseph continued to accuse them, the brothers insisted that they were brothers and their father had sent them in a desperate search for grain. Further questioning revealed that one brother "was no more" and that the youngest had stayed home with their father.

Joseph must have enjoyed seeing his brothers squirm, and some have accused him of playing an elaborate trick on them. But Joseph had every reason to test out the family dynamics with great care. The brothers were imprisoned for three days on charges of spying. This was certainly an opportunity for them to do some serious thinking! Joseph too needed time to process his emotions.

On the third day Joseph, declaring that he too believed in God, agreed to let all but one of them go. The others should take back grain for all their households. One brother would stay behind in prison until Benjamin, the youngest, could be brought to prove the truth of their allegations about the family.

The brothers were thunderstruck. Surely this was a judgment against them for their betrayal of Joseph. Since he had talked with them through an interpreter, they had no idea that he understood what they were saying. "Alas, we are paying the penalty for what we did to our brother; we saw his anguish when he pleaded with us, but we would not listen. That is why this anguish has come upon us."

Reuben retorted, "Did I not tell you not to wrong the boy? But you would not listen. So now there comes a reckoning for his blood" (Genesis 42:21-22). Reuben, however was not innocent. He had never told their father the truth about his favorite son's fate, nor had he made any attempt to rescue Joseph from Egypt.

Tears overwhelmed Joseph when after so many years he knew that his brothers had understood their own responsibility for the terrible crime they had committed. He also understood that the path to reconciliation could not be short or easy. Simeon was tied up while his siblings watched, and he was taken back to prison while the others were sent on their way with grain and with a repayment of the purchase money they had brought. Perhaps some of it had been received years earlier as the price of a slave boy.

As they traveled home, there were questions for the nine brothers to mull. It had been made clear that no more grain would be sold, nor would Simeon be released, until Benjamin's presence verified the claims they had made. Was Simeon to be abandoned in an Egyptian jail as Joseph had been? How deep did the family loyalties lie? The questions were painful, but they brought needed growth. The brothers asked one another, "What is this that God has done to us?" It was a long journey back to their family in Canaan, but the emotional and spiritual distance was even longer.

Old Jacob was beside himself when he learned that Simeon had been detained in Egypt and that only a visit from Benjamin could obtain his release. The viceroy's statement that they would not be free to trade for more grain in Egypt until Benjamin appeared was also a problem. They were all even more alarmed when each man's purchase money appeared in his unloaded sack.

The patriarch now mourned the loss of two sons: Joseph and Simeon. He would not hear of letting Benjamin go to Egypt, for Benjamin and Joseph had been the only children of Jacob's beloved wife Rachel; he could not bear to lose them both.

At last hunger galvanized Reuben into responsible action. "You may kill my two sons if I do not bring [Benjamin] back to you. Put him in my hands, and I will bring him back to you" (Genesis 42:37). There was no other way: the brothers *must* go back to get more grain.

As Jacob continued to protest, Judah stepped forward and promised himself to be the guarantee for Benjamin. "I myself will be surety for him; you can hold me accountable for him. If I do not bring him back to you and set him before you, then let me bear the blame forever" (Genesis 43:9). Though it was Judah's original mean suggestion that had led to Joseph's enslavement, it was his promise now that prompted Jacob to give his consent. A lot of growth was taking place.

The father sent off Benjamin in the company of his brothers with double the money for the purchase of the grain, and eventually they stood again in the presence of Joseph. Again Joseph had to struggle with his emotions, especially at the sight of the beloved Benjamin. It had been at his birth that their mother Rachel had died, and always Joseph had had a special concern for him.

He had the brothers brought to his own house—which only increased their terror. They begged his steward to take the money for their first purchase that they had mysteriously discovered in their sacks. The steward assured them that this must be God's doing, and he brought out Simeon to rejoin them.

On his arrival at the house, Joseph insisted on detailed information about Jacob. Then suddenly he was looking into the eyes of Benjamin. It was more than he could manage, and he left the room hastily to weep in private.

He returned to order a sumptuous feast at which the brothers were given seats according to their birth order. Again they looked at each other in terror: how could this be a coincidence? Benjamin was given extra portions of food.

Afterward they were sent off, again with the money planted in their sacks, and with Joseph's ceremonial cup hidden in the sack of Benjamin. Shortly thereafter officials were sent off to arrest the one who had "taken" the cup.

All the rest of the brothers accompanied Benjamin back to the palace and insisted to Joseph that he was innocent. Joseph said that he had no desire to detain the others, only the guilty party who had stolen his cup.

Judah now took important initiative. He reviewed the whole story of Jacob's distress at releasing his youngest son to go on the journey and how Judah had promised to be accountable for his well-being. The one who had schemed the enslavement of one brother now asked that he be enslaved in place of another. He who had been responsible for bringing their father so much grief now tried desperately to spare him any more. "Now therefore, please let your servant remain as a slave to my lord in place of the boy; and let the boy go back with his brothers. For how can I go back to my father if the boy is not with me? I fear to see the suffering that would come upon my father" (Genesis 44:33-34).

The critical point had come. The repentance was real and over-whelmed Joseph with its completeness. Now a road was open for a deeper reconciliation than he could have imagined. Hastily dismissing his staff, the man so long alienated from his family revealed his true identity. "I am Joseph," he declared.

His brothers could not comprehend, even though he spoke in their own language. At his urging, they came nearer, and Joseph promised that they need not fear vengeance from him. It was God who had been at work to save the family during a terrible famine.

Forgiveness was expressed in generosity. Those who had sold Joseph as a slave were lavishly supplied with food, land and honor in the land of Egypt. They were received in the royal court and showered with favors.

After the death of old Jacob, the brothers were fearful of the resent-ment that Joseph might still hold. He assured them, "Even though you intended to do harm to me, God intended it for good, in order to pre-serve a numerous people, as he is doing today" (Genesis 50:20).

The road to reconciliation had been a long one, but repentance and forgiveness had won. It was the work of God.

HOW CAN I UNDERSTAND
WHAT HELP MY ABUSER NEEDS?

CAROL AND BOB[1] WERE BOTH ACTIVE MEMBERS of First Baptist Church of Greenside Harbor. In fact, they were chosen as delegates for a national church convention, and that is where they reconnected with Rev. George McCullough, a pastor in his mid-thirties who had married them some years back. Now he was called on again to serve as their pastoral counselor, even though they were not members of his church. The story developed like this.

Both Carol and Bob had been married before. Carol had been through a lot of pain and anguish in her first marriage. As a result, she was determined to make sure that her marriage to Bob did not end in failure. But Bob brought a lot of baggage with him into the relationship. Because Bob's divorce had been on the grounds of mental and physical cruelty, the pastor was very reluctant to support his marriage to Carol.

But Bob persisted. He claimed up and down that his old ways had been transformed. He was converted. He'd been saved. The old life was gone. In fact, Bob would quote Scripture to the pastor in support of his newfound life in Christ. "If anyone is in Christ, there is a new creation; everything old has passed away; see, everything has become new!" (2 Corinthians 5:17).

Marrying this couple was a decision that George would later regret. There seemed to be failure all round. In the pastor's own words: "A divorce is a failure, but it's not the person necessarily who has failed, it's the relationship that failed. And maybe who failed . . . is whoever did the wedding." The minister felt great personal responsibility for marrying Bob and Carol. But the religious words Bob spoke had done a snow job on everyone. There seemed to be no way to evaluate his claim of repentance and a new life in Christ.

This story shows the incredible bind Christian victims and their pastors find themselves in when they encounter the persuasive techniques (some would say the manipulation) of a religious abuser. Later, Pastor George would have to face questions from lawyers about why he had agreed to marry Carol and Bob. He would have to stand before the court and acknowledge what happened to Carol as a result of Bob's anger. This Baptist minister would be called on to testify in favor of their divorce, even though he had performed the wedding.

Not surprisingly, Rev. McCullough felt great embarrassment and personal failure as a pastoral counselor as he answered the lawyer in the courtroom. But his desire to support Carol was unwavering. He was determined to testify to the severity of the abuse she had suffered. He wanted Carol to find refuge and freedom before it was too late.

George had to pay close attention to the clues, comments and behavior of Carol and Bob over an extended period of time. He concluded that an abusive man's temporary remorse after a violent incident was insufficient evidence of a commitment to change. Bob acted sorry, but his abusive behavior continued. In spiritual terms, there were no behavioral signs of biblical repentance.

What Is Repentance?

Repentance involves

- a full accounting of the harm that was done

- acknowledging that the behavior was unacceptable
- acknowledging the pain caused by one's behavior
- naming the wrongdoing and recognizing that one is responsible
- humiliation at the memory of one's wrongdoing
- grieving the loss of relationship the behavior has created
- grieving the loss of trust resulting from one's behavior
- grieving the personal cost of one's behavior
- grieving the consequences to others
- recognizing one's lack of inner resources to make amends
- recognizing one's failed relationship with God, and perhaps with the church
- deciding that the future will be different from the past
- deciding that the future will involve new plans and new ways of behaving
- hungering for a renewed connection to God, born out of personal failure
- a plan of action to change
- asking others to help carry out this plan of action
- forming strategies for accountability
- following through on the plans and strategies for change
- changing one's behavior

Repentance is a biblical term for the deep sorrow of a person who has wronged someone else. It involves emotional turmoil and an explicit resolve not to act in the same way again. Jesus' story of the tax collector and the Pharisee, recorded in Luke 18:10-14, pictures the one who is repenting as saying heartfelt words and casting down his eyes. In the case of Zacchaeus, his repentant heart led immediately to changed behavior: he paid back fourfold all those from whom he had stolen.

Repentance is *not*

- measured by how much emotion the abuser shows, how many tears he sheds
- measured by the extravagance of the gifts the abuser gives
- measured by the eloquence of the words he uses to say "I'm sorry"
- scheduled by anyone other than the abuser
- a process that can be demanded
- an act that the church's rules can require
- a manipulation of the Christian community to pretend that everything will now be OK
- a return to normal, everyday living as if the abuse never happened

It is not easy to tell when true repentance has occurred. But there are clues. True repentance bears fruit. There will be evidence of changed behavior. Still, change takes place slowly. It comes as the result of hard work and supportive counsel. Justice and accountability are central ingredients in an abuser's journey toward real change. They require time, and normally the process requires many steps.

For the cycle of violence to be broken, effective services must be available to help men on their road to accountability, justice, healing and wholeness. Often there is ongoing monitoring to ensure safety for the woman and accountability for the man. For many men, involvement in an abusers group is an important means of change.

THE ROLE OF BATTERERS INTERVENTION PROGRAMS

"I am not violent!" These are sometimes the first words that come out of the mouth of an abuser as he begins a program for male batterers. He says this despite the police reports of force, the emergency room visits of his victim, the fear of his children and his criminal record of assault.

"I am violent no longer!" These are the words group facilitators long to hear. With the support of a trained counselor and an environment that encourages altered behavior, some abusive men come to a point where they take responsibility for the violence they have committed in the past and show remorse for their actions and empathy for their victims. As a result, they alter both their attitudes and their conduct. In these cases, their participation in the program has been successful: change has occurred.

Predicting *when* and *if* the violence will stop in the life of an abuser is extremely difficult. Many women victims persist in clinging to the promise and hope of change in a violent man they love. Some are bitterly disappointed.

What is a program for male batterers? Programs for men who batter have begun to appear across North America because of increasing concern for victim safety and protection. To some degree, these programs are an alternative to incarceration, and many judges now order attendance at such groups as part of the sentencing of an abuser. Intervention programs also offer hope for women victims who do not want to end the relationship with their abusive husband but who desperately want the violence to stop. So whether or not batterers' programs are effective is of interest to a broad range of people and institutions—the justice system, psychologists and social workers, and most especially women, like you, who have been victimized.

Is my abuser likely to complete a program if he begins it? Completion rates vary dramatically across the United States and Canada. The likelihood of remaining in the program or of dropping out is related to such things as age, marital status, employment, motivation to attend and complete the intervention program, and the frequency and severity of the abusive acts. In a project of one Christian program for men who batter, we found that when the pastor sends an abuser to the program, or when his wife requires him to attend, the man is more likely to complete the intervention program than if his attendance was mandated by a judge.[2]

Never underestimate how important it is to insist that your partner seek help. And if you can encourage your pastor to do likewise, so much the better.

Do batterer intervention programs work? Batterer intervention programs have two goals: (1) victim safety and (2) rehabilitating the abuser, particularly stopping the violence. It is urgently important to know whether these programs are effective. Why? First, courts are more frequently sending batterers to intervention programs, which implies, at least indirectly, confidence that they work.[3] Second, and more important, these programs offer hope to women like you that their partner's violent behavior can be changed.[4]

Evaluating whether an intervention program for batterers is effective is complicated.[5] The critical issue, the gold standard by which any program's effectiveness must be assessed, is the safety of the victim. But obtaining victim reports is not easy or straightforward. A program's success also depends partly on the abuser's situation: Has the court ordered him to attend the program? Has he been held accountable for his past behavior? Has he done anything violent since entering the program? Has his behavior changed? Have his attitudes toward women, or violence, changed? A third issue has to do with other serious problems, such as unemployment, substance abuse, mental health disorders, in the life of a man who has abused his wife.

All of these issues make it very hard to evaluate whether an intervention program is effective and what is its rate of success in changing violent behavior. Obviously, these programs focus on the men's accountability to each other and to the facilitators. Yet these programs do not have either the legal ability or the resources to *enforce* accountability. They are simply one of many resources needed to end domestic violence.

A book published decades ago, *Behind Closed Doors*, argued that the lower a husband's economic resources and social prestige in comparison to his wife's, the greater his tendency to use physical force to gain or maintain a dominant power position within the family.[6] Since that time, other researchers have found that negative work experiences for men are linked with abusive acts against their wife or girlfriend. Contrary to conventional wisdom, excessive alcohol consumption hasn't been shown, by itself, to be a main culprit. Men who abuse their wife while drinking heavily also abuse her when sober. However, many abusive men blame their violence on alcohol. Some researchers have argued that wife abusers get drunk deliberately in order to carry out a premeditated violent act.

In this chapter we highlight some of the spiritual resources that can assist in a male abuser's process of change. Such change is very, very difficult, and intervention programs for batterers, anger management training, and individual psychotherapy are all important. Spiritual resources cannot substitute for justice, and we certainly aren't suggesting that instant cures are available. But for Christian families, there are biblical resources that can help alongside therapy and community programs. Stories from Scripture help to give Christians hope.

Joseph, after being traumatized by his brothers' violence, went on to be an instrument of healing as he called them to accountability. Justice and accountability are central to the Scripture's call to change. Remorse and attempts at restoration do not erase the harm that has been done. Paul could not bring back to life people he had killed; yet he continually gathered gifts to bring as peace offerings to the believers in Jerusalem whom he had once terrorized and persecuted (see 1 Timothy 1:12-14).

It is important to remember that many batterers have been abused themselves. Often they witnessed or experienced violence in their childhood home. While as adults they may *excuse* or *justify* their violent behavior[7]—and it is inexcusable and unjustifiable—men who are abusive are often hurting. Wrongs against them in the past may never have been properly identified or treated; as a result, these men carry scars and vulnerabilities from their childhood and youth.

If the courts in this land can mandate treatment for abusers, why can't their wives? In fact, we have heard the phrase "wife-mandated treatment" used for an abused woman's insistence that her abusive husband seek help and that if he does not, she will leave the home and the marriage. She is holding him accountable for his behavior. But whether he is willing to seek help is up to him.

You cannot accept responsibility for your husband's decision. What *you* must accept responsibility for is ensuring your own safety and that of your children.

WHAT IS GOD'S PATTERN FOR A HUSBAND'S BEHAVIOR?

Both the Old and New Testaments give us pictures. Isaiah 54 pictures God as the husband of Israel, who has been anything but a perfect wife. Nevertheless, here is the behavior that God promises her, and surely it is a pattern for husbands.

The *Word in Life Study Bible* analyzes the passage and comes up with the following portrait of a godly husband. He is one who

- helps his wife find fulfillment (54:1-3)
- seeks to allay her fears (54:4, 14,15)
- builds up her reputation (54:4)
- displays godly character toward his partner (54:4)
- does not allow prolonged conflict or lingering anger to keep him separated from his wife (54:6-8)
- replaces anger with kindness (54:9-10)
- brings comfort in the midst of stress (54:11-12)
- instructs the couple's children in spiritual matters (54:13)
- protects his wife from dangers and threats (54:16-17)

    Isaiah 62:1-5 offers another view of the bridegroom's treatment of his bride.

- He protects and purifies her.
- He honors and values her.
- He identifies himself with her, as signified by giving her new names.[8]

    The New Testament speaks of Christ as the bridegroom who gave his life for his bride, the church, so that she might come to fulfillment, "holy and without blemish" (Ephesians 5:27). A husband is to cherish his wife's body and mind as he does his own (Ephesians 5:28-29) and see that she suffers no harm.

WHAT IS THE BIBLICAL PATTERN FOR A GODLY WIFE?
She is characterized by strength and honor, by her ability to make good decisions and the loving care she gives to her family. She is fully mature, able to contribute to the family's financial needs and able to act independently. Not only does she understand her own worth, but she is respected in the community and loved by her husband and children (see Proverbs 31:10-31). St. Peter says, "Let your adornment be the inner self with the lasting beauty of a gentle and quiet spirit, which is very precious in God's sight" (1 Peter 3:4).

WHY DON'T THE LEADERS IN MY CHURCH TEACH THIS?
They may just be following what they have heard others say, or they may be misunderstanding or distorting what the Scriptures have to say about marriage (see 2 Peter 3:16). Your call is to follow the words of Scripture rather than of those who are misled.

> *Why won't they listen to me or help me?*
> *Who rises up for me against the wicked?*
> *Who stands up for me against evildoers? (Psalm 94:16)*

> *Again I saw all the oppressions that are practiced under the sun. Look, the tears of the oppressed—with no one to comfort them! On the side of their oppressors there was power—with no one to comfort them. (Ecclesiastes 4:1)*

> *The LORD saw it, and it displeased him*
> *that there was no justice.*
> *He saw that there was no one,*
> *and was appalled that there was no one to intervene. (Isaiah 59:15-16)*

A CAUTIOUS PATH TO FORGIVENESS AND RECONCILIATION

The early church in Jerusalem had been devastated by Saul of Tarsus. The Scriptures tell us that he was the ringleader of a great persecution. Going from house to house in his wild rage against the church, he dragged off both men and women and took them to prison. He was a very ugly perpetrator, driven both by religious fanaticism and personal fury, "breathing out threats and slaughter."

But as he was on his way to do more violence against the church, Christ met him and transformed him. He was now Paul the servant of Christ—but how was he to make reconciliation with the church, and how were the believers to forgive him? When he made his first visit to Jerusalem after his conversion, the apostles were fearful and suspicious. "He attempted to join the disciples; and they were all afraid of him, for they did not believe that he was a disciple" (Acts 9:26). How could they be sure that his repentance and transformation were real? If they received him, would they be putting the household of God at risk? They also had to deal with their anger against the one who had wreaked so much harm among them.

Barnabas, whose name meant "Son of Encouragement," was able to get beyond his resentment and give Paul an opportunity to demonstrate his new heart. Quite privately, Barnabas escorted him to an interview with James and Peter (Acts 9:27; Galatians 1:18-19). Peter, though a victim of persecution himself, was willing to receive Paul into his home—a decided risk, since this zealot had previously entered numerous Christian homes to drag the residents away to their death. But Paul was not allowed to see the other apostles. In point of fact, it was many years before the church of Judea laid eyes on him (Galatians 1:22-24), though they were informed that "the one who persecuted us is now proclaiming the faith."

Little by little, Paul was able to demonstrate the reality of his repentance. He was able to confess his crimes and to take responsibility for them (Acts 22:4; 26:9-11; 1 Corinthians 15:9). More than once he

Abusers' statements that worry abuse victims . . .

(Perhaps you have heard several of them over the years. Perhaps you could add others to the list.)

God is still changing me. Don't be impatient.

Everyone deserves another chance.

You hurt me too!

Be thankful that I'm not as harsh as I used to be.

Get over it.

Stop thinking about the past.

I didn't mean to injure you.

You weren't listening to me. Otherwise I wouldn't have hit you.

Stop crying. I didn't hit you that hard.

I said I was sorry. What more do you want?

Where is the nice, happy girl I married?

brought funds for famine relief to Jerusalem (Acts 11:3; 12:25; 24:17; Romans 15:25-28, 31; 1 Corinthians 16:1-4, 15; 2 Corinthians 8:1-4; Galatians 2:10). There he engaged Greek Jews in dialogue and argued the claims of Christ until his own life was endangered (Acts 9:29-30). When the Christians saw his willingness to take the risk, they arranged for his escape.

There came a time when Paul was summoned to explain his ministry before the Jerusalem Council, and they heard his wonderful account with joy (Acts 15:12; see also Acts 21:17-19). They affirmed his call to

bring the gospel to Gentiles but asked that he always remember to do
what he could to alleviate the suffering that he himself had occasioned
in Jerusalem (Galatians 2:10). He could not bring back those whom he
had murdered nor restore property that had been seized, but he did all
that he could to make amends for the mischief he had caused.

In the end, homes opened to him, and he was welcomed where once
he had been shunned. The saints who had been rightfully reserved now
opened their hearts to him. He had proved his repentance, and the believers received him warmly as one of their own. It was a long process,

Abusers' statements that give abuse victims cause for hope . . .

I don't want to hurt you anymore.

I am sorry for causing you so much pain.

I clearly went over the line.

When you're ready, I would like to talk to you again.

I want to love you without trying to control you.

I should never have threatened to hurt you.

I understand why you were frightened of me.

I have repented of my abusive behavior. Now I want to
change the way I act.

I want us to make decisions together from now on.

Perhaps you need more time before I contact you again.

Although it's very hard for me to go each week, I am
committed to completing the treatment program.

but a glorious one that could be neither rushed nor thwarted.

The soul of an abused woman needs to be nourished. Such nourishment is far more important than gifts of flowers or diamonds. There are some basic things you need if you are to move on in your relationship with a man who once abused you. You need to feel stronger, safe to voice your own opinions, able to live without the fear or the threat of violence. You need to be valued for who you are, respected for your skills and talents. You need to be able to take advantage of the opportunities that are presented to you (even by the abuser) without feeling any obligation to reconcile. As the story of Joseph and his brothers shows, it takes a long time to demonstrate good faith. Pastoral help and a believing community can help you in this process. But the ultimate decision about reconciliation is yours alone to make.

The Holy Spirit will empower you. Like Rizpah, you can stand for what is right. Like Abigail, you can take prompt and decisive action when you need to. Like Esther, you can gain authority in your own fight and in so doing empower other women too.

Ultimately you can call your abusive partner to accountability. You can insist that he seek help. But it is not your responsibility to make sure that he does so. If he is unwilling to seek help or to change his abusive ways, you must protect yourself and the children under your care. Do you have to continue to live in fear? No. "God has not given the spirit of fear but of power and love and balanced judgment" (2 Timothy 1:7, our translation).

FOR SPIRITUAL REFLECTION

Is the man supposed to be the boss of the family? The only place where the Bible says that "every man should be master in his own house" is in the book of Esther (Esther 1:22). This statement was a decree of an irresponsible pagan king, Ahasuerus, who made a number of very bad decisions.

The story starts when he hosts an enormous drinking party in the midst of which he demands that the queen show off her charms, wearing only her royal crown, before the drunken mob. Clearly this is a case of wife abuse. In that culture, shame and honor were critically important in any evaluation of women. The king is trying to force his wife into a publicly humiliating action, one that will permanently deprive her of honor in both her own eyes and the eyes of the king's subjects. Certainly there is no concern for her feelings or personal dignity.

Vashti, the queen, maintains her dignity by refusing to violate her own modesty and self-respect. She simply will not display her body before the most influential governors of the empire; she will not sacrifice her honor and that of her family. The choice is costly, for she loses her position as queen.

The king is enraged when his command is denied. He calls a consultation of his officials, and one of them, Memucan, complains that Vashti's refusal to obey has created a problem for the whole realm. Some of its influential citizens feel severely threatened.

> This deed of the queen will be made known to all women, causing them to look with contempt on their husbands, since they will say, "King Ahasuerus commanded Queen Vashti to be brought before him, and she did not come." This very day the noble ladies of Persia and Media who have heard of the queen's behavior will rebel against the king's officials, and there will be no end of contempt and wrath! (Esther 1:17-18)

Then King Ahasuerus starts a search for a new wife and creates special far-reaching legislation: "He [the king] sent letters to all the royal provinces, to every province in its own script and to every people in its own language, declaring that every man should be master in his own house" (Esther 1:22).

Here is a mandate that does encourage wife abuse, and it occurs *only here* in the Bible—not as a command of God but as the command of a pagan king. The text tells us that this decree was intended to subjugate every woman in the kingdom (Esther 1:20)—and the law of the Medes and Persians could not be changed. Thus women are now vulnerable to any outrage their husbands might devise.

These are the conditions of the Persian Empire when Esther, a young Jewish woman, enters the palace and is ultimately crowned as queen. Her position is not one to be envied, for her husband is cruel and capricious. In return for a large bribe from his prime minister, he agrees to sign an order that all Jews in the empire are to be killed. Ahasuerus seems to have little concern for the victims; apparently he doesn't even realize their identity nor the value of the leadership their nation has supplied in the empire.

Then Esther understands that she must ask to save her people, even at the risk of her own life. Throughout the story, two themes are woven. One is the threat to the survival of the entire Hebrew population, the other is the threat to the happiness and welfare of women. Using her wits, her beauty and the prayers of the believing community, Esther devises a plan to lessen the effect of both of the king's decrees. Since the decrees have been made law, they cannot be changed, but their effects can be much diminished.

The story is a long and lively one, with many ups and downs. Although the name of God is never mentioned in this biblical book, that name does appear four times as an acrostic at critical points.[9] Katharine Bushnell provided translations that enable the English reader to see how the name of the Lord is hidden in key sentences. She maintains that in this way we may see God at work backstage even when the unbelieving Gentiles of the Persian Empire are unaware of it.[10]

After a period of fasting and prayer, Esther enters the king's presence unbidden. To do so, she must break several of the empire's laws. No one was supposed to approach the king unless he had called for them. For Esther to come before the throne without invitation is an act of civil disobedience—and of marital disobedience as well. This does not stop the courageous queen who must plead for her people.

She is clever enough not to reveal her concern at first; instead she stirs up the king's curiosity with an invitation to two successive dinner parties. The tone of the king begins to change. He does not demand that she state her wish but begs her to tell him her desire. The formerly cruel and callous husband is now intrigued by what may be going on in his wife's mind.

Now she brings forth her desperate petition, pleading for the lives of her people. She points out that the king himself will suffer great loss if he is deprived of the abilities and responsible citizenship of the Jews. When Ahasuerus realizes that he has been tricked into enacting a really terrible law, he stomps off in rage.

The execution of his prime minister, Haman, follows swiftly, but nothing has yet been done to prevent the destruction of the Hebrews. The law still stands.

Again Esther must risk her life to come before the king. Again she must plead for a revoking of the decree that her husband had foolishly issued. Ahasuerus simply passes on the responsibility to Esther and her uncle, Mordecai. It is up to them to figure out how to do damage control. "You may write as you please with regard to the Jews, in the name of the king, and seal it with the king's ring; for an edict written in the name of the king and sealed with the king's ring cannot be revoked" (Esther 8:8).

The once powerless woman now has power to check the evil that was planned, and to do so in the name of the king. The king's scribes are called, and royal decrees are sent forth announcing that the Jews living in the empire are to take up arms in their own defense if any should attack them. Not only is there rejoicing among the Jews, but many become converts to Judaism (Esther 8:17). Esther's faith has led others to a faith in the true and living God.

On the appointed day, the Jews gather to defend themselves, and there is a great slaughter of those who sought their ruin. Ahasuerus gives his wife a progress report and asks, "Now what is your petition? It shall be granted you. And what further is your request? It shall be fulfilled" (9:12). Far from being indifferent to his wife's wishes, he seeks her out to learn what more he can do to be helpful. This time it is he that initiates the approach. Their marriage is taking on completely new dimensions, becoming a partnership. The tyrant is making important discoveries!

Esther, having her own sources of information, requests permission for the defense of the Jews to be continued for one further day in the capital city. The permission is granted, and the deliverance of the Jews throughout the entire empire becomes secure. Now Esther sends a directive to them "with full written authority" (9:29) that these two days should be commemorated each year. "The command of Queen Esther fixed these practices of Purim, and it was recorded in writing" (9:32).

Not only has Esther gained authority in her own right, but she has empowered all the women of the realm as well. She has spoken with her own voice, and the king has listened. He has learned from the wisdom and courage of one woman—and that reality cannot be concealed from either men or women. The decree that devalued women has been replaced by an affirmation of the heroism and faith of a woman whose fame lives on today, far after the fall of her husband's empire and its laws. She resisted the injustice and violence in her own day, and we cannot mistake her continuing message to us.

🌹

Few brides have had a more unhappy ending to their wedding night than did Leah. As morning broke, her husband Jacob realized that he was not lying beside Rachel, the lovely woman for whom he had labored so long. Instead he was gazing at her older sister, Leah.

He had come to the home of her family seven years prior, fleeing the anger of his older brother whom he had tricked out of both his birthright and their father's blessing. In danger of his life, he had been sent by his mother to find safety with her brother, Laban. The fugitive had first seen Rachel at the village well as he arrived to seek the home of her father, and she had joyfully welcomed her newfound cousin.

For seven long years Jacob worked as his uncle's herdsman to earn the bride price for Rachel, "and they seemed to him but a few days because of the love he had for her" (Genesis 29:20). For seven years he yearned for her, waiting to possess his beloved. Now, instead of the consummation of his longing, Jacob the trickster had been tricked by his own uncle. The wrong woman was in his bed. The truth was that Leah had been used as a pawn. The father had palmed off the daughter on a most unwilling husband.

Jacob went off angrily to confront Laban, who observed that it was necessary for the older sister to be married first. But if Jacob would do his husbandly duty with Leah for one week, he might then be married to the younger sister. In exchange, he must work a second seven years.

And so the week was completed, but only grudgingly. Leah was an unloved wife, having little power. Both she and Jacob had been betrayed by her father, and she was left with no sense of self-worth, more a possession than a person.

Jacob poured the ardor of his soul into his union with Rachel. Perhaps the most positive thing that can be said about him is his unwavering devotion throughout his life to the woman he adored. The delight that he took in her, however, underlined his resentment over the other wife whom he had been forced to accept.

Although her circumstances were tragic, Leah soon knew the satisfaction of life stirring within her. She had conceived, while Rachel had not, and she hoped to win her husband's love by presenting him with this child. The Bible says, "When the LORD saw that Leah was unloved, he opened her womb" (Genesis 29:31). God cared for Leah, making her fruitful. The child was a boy named Reuben, meaning "God has seen my misery." But Jacob's love could not be won, even with the gift of his first son.

Leah's prayer life deepened, and her second son was named Simeon, "God who hears." She said, "Because the LORD has heard that I am hated, he has given me this son also" (Genesis 29:33). Increasingly she turned to God. Though her circumstances were bitter, her confidence in God's loving care was strong.

When her third son was born, she declared with pathetic hope, "Now this time my husband will be joined to me, because I have borne him three sons" (29:34). And so the third child was named Levi, "attached." Her hope proved vain, but her relationship with God grew. The next son was named Judah, "praise," for she said, "This time I will praise the LORD." In the midst of a painful personal tragedy, she was still able to praise.

But her sister Rachel grew increasingly bitter because she had no children, until in desperation she gave her slave girl to Jacob as a concubine. According to the laws of that society, any children who were conceived would be accounted as the sons or daughters of the mistress. This resulted in the birth of two sons, Dan and Naphtali. Their names express the animosity that raged between the two sisters. At the birth of Dan, "he has vindicated," Rachel announced, "God has judged me, and has also heard my voice and given me a son." The second name, Naphtali ("my struggle"), displays the meanness of her spirit as she announced "With mighty wrestlings I have wrestled with my sister, and have prevailed" (Genesis 30:1-8).

Not to be outdone, Leah too gave her serving maid to Jacob as a concubine and gained the credit for two more sons: Gad ("good fortune") and Asher ("happy"). She had won in the baby-making race, but not in gaining the affection of her husband.

Since he would not come to her willingly, she resorted to bartering with her sister for Jacob's sexual services. Meeting him in the field, Leah directed, "You must come in to me; for I have hired you." Despite the humiliating circumstances, "God heeded Leah, and she conceived and bore Jacob a fifth son." She named him Issachar, "reward," because "God has given me my hire because I gave my maid to my husband." Again she recognized God's hand in her life, and at the birth of her sixth son, she declared, "God has endowed me with a good dowry; now my husband will honor me, because I have borne him six sons." The child was named Zebulon ("honor"; Genesis 30:14-20).

Leah is a prototype of women whose most valiant efforts bring little response. Over the years, the rivalry grew less intense as Rachel herself at last had a son. The relationship with Laban, however, deteriorated until Jacob decided to leave with his family and flocks. For the first time since Bethel, we are told that he listened to God's voice (Genesis 31:3). Jacob sent for both of his wives to explain his reasons and to have them prepare to leave. For the first time we read of his treating them equally rather than with pronounced favoritism (see Genesis 31:4-16).

The sisters stand together in insisting that they as well as their husband have been unfairly treated by their father. They agree to sneak away while Laban is off shearing sheep.

The father catches up with the runaways and insists that Jacob must treat both of his daughters properly. "The LORD watch between you and me, when we are absent one from another. If you ill-treat my daughters, or if you take wives in addition to my daughters, though no one else is with us, remember that God is witness between you and me" (Genesis 31:49-50).

How often the first part of this "Mizpah" benediction is used to close youth meetings or worship services, and yet originally it was given as a protection against the abuse of two wives. Leah was beginning to be respected as a full person, worthy of dignity and honor equally with her younger sister.

Now Jacob must face the consequences of the way he had treated his brother Esau twenty years earlier. Would he still seek revenge for what Jacob had done to him? Jacob sent his wives and children across the brook Jabbok while he remained alone in the camp. Mysteriously, a stranger appeared and engaged the troubled Jacob in hand-to-hand combat. All night long they wrestled, with neither gaining the upper hand. Though the stranger inflicted an injury on Jacob's hip, Jacob's arms still held his opponent firmly. He sensed that the wrestler was a spiritual being, and his resistance to God's ways was coming to an end. "I will not let you go, unless you bless me" (Genesis 32:26).

That blessing changed his name from Jacob the cheater to Israel, prince or struggler with God. "For," the stranger added, "you have striven with God and with humans, and have prevailed" (32:28). Now Jacob realized that his encounter had been with God and that, like Hagar's, his life had been spared. This was the beginning of his transformation.

As Jacob's family later approached Esau, the concubines and their children were placed first in a more vulnerable position, then the family of Leah, and last—in the safest place—Rachel and Joseph. The meeting with Esau actually brought reconciliation and a welcome for his wives and children.

In the new land Rachel died while giving birth to Benjamin, and she was buried at Bethlehem (35:16-20). Though he continued to grieve for her and to favor her children, the transformed Israel now looked at Leah with new eyes. The struggler with God was being transformed.

Now she assumed the status of first wife, for when Joseph bragged of his dream of the sun, moon and eleven stars bowing to him, Jacob retorted, "Shall we indeed come, I and your mother and your brothers, and bow to the ground before you?" (37:10). The mother was clearly Leah, since Rachel was already dead. Jacob had become protective of Leah's place of honor in the family. The despised wife was now defended.

At Leah's death, she was laid to rest along with her husband's ancestors, with full recognition of her as chief wife of the father of the clan. When Jacob came to the end of his life, it was not beside Rachel that he asked to be buried but rather beside Leah (Genesis 49:31). The unloved wife had come into her own.

– Eight –

HOW DO I LEARN
TO TRUST GOD AGAIN?

WHEN JESUS HEALED SOMEONE, it was common for him to say, "Your faith has made you whole." Sometimes it was the faith of a family member or a friend that was instrumental in the healing process, but most often it was the trust of the sick or disabled themselves. The story of the healing of blind Bartimaeus (Mark 10:46-52) offers us an interesting look into the relationship between faith and action in the life of a person asking for a touch from God.

Bartimaeus was sitting by the side of the road outside the city gates. Noise growing in the distance let him know that a crowd was approaching. Crowds were good news for persons who begged, because the passing of many people brought the possibility of extra donations.

But this was not any ordinary crowd; these were men and women following Jesus, the rabbi known for his remarkable teaching and powers of healing. Bartimaeus began to shout, "Jesus, son of David, have mercy on me!" The crowds rebuked him. "Shhhhh!" Their manner was curt: the rabbi is not interested in you. But Bartimaeus called out even more loudly, oblivious to their wish that he remain silent.

The rabbi stopped, responsive to the cries of one who could not see.

Then Jesus did a curious thing: he asked the crowds to call Bartimaeus to come. "Get up, he is calling you," they said. Casting his cloak aside, Bartimaeus approached the One who could alter his fate by touch or the spoken word.

This story gives us many insights into the link between healing and human action. The crowd at first tried to shush the beggar. He had to continue to call out for help, despite the lack of support from the rabbi's followers. When Jesus summoned him, the blind beggar cast aside his only possession, the cloak that gave him shade by day from the sun and warmth by night.[1]

The Bible does not hide the fact that individuals and their families go through difficulties. In fact, Scripture is full of examples of families in crisis, in abuse, and in heartache and despair. It is also clear that a spiritual response to crisis begins with recognizing one's need for help, as we discussed in chapter one. *How do I know that I need help?* You know you need help if you are living in fear, constantly walking on eggshells and being deeply hurt by someone you love. When your physical or mental health cannot be assured in your home, it is time to get help. Individual responsibility is central.

Once you are determined to seek healing and wholeness, you will need to decide how much of your story to tell and to whom. As we discussed in chapter two, you alone control the silence of your suffering. Choosing to break that silence involves reflecting on how much pain you have suffered, remembering your partner's broken promises, considering how much fear you feel, and realizing that your children's lives are affected too. Take courage. There is hope for a life free of abuse.

In chapter three we outlined some of the spiritual needs you may have as you journey toward wholeness. In chapter four we pointed the way to community resources. Chapters five and six talked about getting started on the journey and the key steps you will need to take in order to get on with your life. And in chapter seven we looked at some of the resources available to assist abusive men who are willing to seek help.

We also discussed the important Christian value of forgiveness and the part it plays in recovery.

THE POWER OF FAITH

God's involvement in human suffering is vividly displayed in many passages of the Old and New Testaments—maybe most clearly in Jesus' experience in the Garden of Gethsemane. Here, just before his betrayal with a kiss of greeting from Judas, Jesus prayed to God for strength. Just a few steps away were the sleeping disciples. The Garden of Gethsemane offered shade from the heat and rest from the crowds. It was the place where Jesus often went to rest. In the safety and privacy of the garden, Judas knew Jesus would be the most vulnerable.

To us Gethsemane represents pain and anguish, but it also offers hope, renewal and power to overcome. To find the inner strength to leave the garden and begin journeying toward healing is never easy. Working through the pain, the betrayal and the shattered dreams, you can move from being a victim to being a survivor. The term *victim* highlights the abuse a woman has suffered, but *survivor* places our focus on the skills and inner resources women develop in order to move forward. In our research, women use both terms to refer to themselves, reflecting not only their past experiences but also their present realities. The Garden of Gethsemane reminds us that *spiritual* strength is available to those who call, even when the community of believers around us is fast asleep, oblivious to our need for help.

Meditation on Scripture can give you a framework to place around your personal suffering. You may find inspiration in the Israelites' long journey from slavery to freedom. Or you may want to focus on Jesus' life, with its betrayal, humiliation and suffering followed by victory. In true stories like these, believers encounter a great source of strength that helps them overcome enormous affliction. Even in deep suffering, there is hope. After the darkness of death and slavery comes the promise of new life and freedom. Transformation and healing are central to the biblical account: with God's presence and power, it is possible to overcome. Painful experiences of the body and the spirit are never to be diminished or denied, but they can be transformed and overcome by the power of healing love. This is the gospel message.

How does faith make a battered woman strong? Biblical stories and faith in God help to ease the pain believers face. This is the message we have been given by Christian women who have survived abuse in the family. This can be your testimony too. Through the years we have heard many abused women say, "My faith has made me strong."[2] Faith in God can give you strength when you need it most.

How does our faith make us strong when we feel weak inside? What is the process? Here are some of the lessons that abused women (or the spiritual leaders who have helped them) learned and shared with Nancy and her research team.[3]

- Faith makes a victim strong when her church or faith community condemns the abuse.

- The role of the church and the pastor is to be God's representative, and certainly God is not happy with family violence.

- Faith strengthens her when another believer shares a personal story of abuse.

- It's in sharing one on one the pain and knowing the hope that you have reached or attained a certain place . . . just hearing someone else's story. . . . Sharing the pain as well as the hope sometimes will lift the burden.

- Faith gives her strength when others in the faith community offer a listening ear.

- I think, Listen, let them vent, don't pass an opinion, encourage them to seek help . . .

- Faith makes her strong when others in the faith community offer practical support.

- I think there's a very definite role . . . yet not only in the listening . . . help with the care of children and all the practical food and shelter needs; I think that women have a very large role to play.

- Faith gives her strength when her faith community looks out for the needs of her children.

- She needs to know that there are choices. . . . Also for the children's sake, if the woman's being abused and she has no outlet for support, she might take it out on her kids 'cause she feels . . . trapped.

- Faith is a source of strength when her faith community builds bridges to needed services.

- Women have a wonderful networking system.

- Faith sometimes grows in adversity.

- I think that God doesn't want these things to happen to me, but I think that they happen anyway for a whole variety of reasons . . . but I think that he allows them to happen in the sense that OK, you're in this situation, let's make it into a positive situation by making it a learning experience and a growing experience. . . . And that's been the way I have reconciled what has happened in my own life.

- Faith gives spiritual tools to assist in a time of crisis.

- The spiritual side of things is overlooked in the secular . . . a need that some people need to get complete healing . . . the power of prayer, a spirit of reconciliation, and forgiveness . . . and forgiveness in that situation so that she can carry on and not have that load, with or without the man.

- Prayer is the language of faith.

- The Lord showed me in my prayer time in 1980 that I had to take control of my life . . .

- Faith strengthens the abuse survivor when the faith community offers her the opportunity to tell her story of abuse.

- The first time that I shared publicly my testimony . . . that was a healing thing. . . . You feel shamed to have been abused. . . . I think women need to become healed enough that they can share so that they can help others, but it takes time. I mean, it took me eight or nine years.

As you can see, women certainly have stories to tell of how their faith made them strong through the crisis and the pain they were suffering. God gave some the courage to leave an abusive home temporarily, or forever. Others gained strength to seek help. For most, faith offered an oasis in the desert, a time to reflect on God's design for peaceful living, a needed contrast to their own suffering and abuse. Many abused Christian women experienced a spiritual awakening: the inconsistency between the gospel message of peace and their own life of fear and turmoil led them to action.

You too can take that step. You too can start on the journey of healing and of hope.

DEALING WITH YOUR ANGER

While you are on the journey, there may be periods when you feel mad at God. At these times you are filled with questions like, Why me? What did I do to deserve this? Why am I not being rescued?

Remember that God is not the instigator of violence, abuse or oppression.

> You are not a God who delights in wickedness;
>   evil will not sojourn with you.
> The boastful will not stand before your eyes;
>   you hate all evildoers.
> You destroy those who speak lies;
>   the LORD abhors the bloodthirsty and deceitful. (Psalm 5:4-6)

God does not condone violence or abuse; the Bible is full of statements condemning oppression of every kind. But people are given free choice over their own actions, and all too often they make the wrong choice, one that gives them power over other human beings. Nevertheless, when God speaks to Israel as his wife, he promises: "If anyone stirs up strife, it is not from me; whoever stirs up strife with you shall fail because of you. . . . No weapon that is fashioned against you shall prosper" (Isaiah 54:15, 17).

Your anger toward those in the Christian church who misled you may be justified. As we have pointed out before, victims do not always find help in their own faith community. They may be shamed, reproached, ignored or told to go back to a dangerous situation. It is very hard to be rejected in the time of deepest need.

Jesus told a story of two respected religious leaders who simply walked by on the other side of the road when they saw a man lying beaten, half dead. It was a member of a different community who rescued the victim, tended his wounds and took him to a safe place. There *are* godly people waiting to do that for you. There are people to whom God is speaking about just such needs as yours. There are many women and men committed to helping victims of abuse, just like you.

The Lord is famous for delivering people from oppression. The Bible promises "a way of escape" (1 Corinthians 10:13), and we encourage you to believe that promise. But a "way out" still means action: you have to walk through it. There are many possibilities for you to consider: the listening ear of a friend, a prayer and support group, a hotline, a wise counselor, a batterers' intervention group, a safe house or shelter, counseling services from a community agency.

God's plan is that there should be peace and safety in your home (see our appendix on peace). He does not call you to live in an abusive situation. Now is the time for faith and action.

HEALING INSIGHTS
Pastors and other Christian leaders who have supported women, children and families seeking spiritual help have wise insights into the link between faith and healing. Where is God in the midst of smashed

dreams and broken human spirits? What is a divine touch? Here is how some of them respond to questions like these.[4]

- Faith in God is an integral part of the mending process.
  I think that, yes, God can take care of all your problems, but I think he's also given us all kinds of tools to help ourselves and to better ourselves. . . . There comes a point in time, I think, when we say that God can put back together what man can tear apart.

- A woman's spiritual life is affected by the abuse—and by her decision to seek help.
  She reclaimed her faith. . . . God was going to be a big help to her in maintaining her semblance of sanity and ability to cope. . . . It was successful from her viewpoint. Unfortunately it resulted in a divorce court, but she didn't give up. So it taught her a lot of spiritual skills like perseverance and trust in God and things like that. So for her spiritual growth . . . it was definitely a bonus.

- Sometimes there is healing of the relationship.
  To me, it brings a lot of satisfaction to see broken marriages healed, because I really firmly believe that's God's will for his people.

- Sometimes abusive men blame the church and clergy for the abuse.
  He actually blames the church and me for the change in his wife. . . . Since making her commitment, she tried to live a different lifestyle, and he doesn't see that as being positive. . . . [There has been] a very spiritual struggle for her to maintain her Christian commitment, even though they're separated.

- God can lead you to a supportive network and a caring pastor.
  I never say that I recommend for you to get divorced; I would understand if they felt they had to. But I would also state that it's a . . . decision that you have to determine for yourself and we will try and support you as best we can. But I would not come out and say, "Go and divorce him."

When ministers recognize that abuse—not divorce—destroys a marriage, they are much more able to assist battered women. In fact, among a small group of once-abused women who had been free of abuse for at least one year after they sought help, many claimed that it was their pastor who helped them understand that safety is essential and even divorce is acceptable for a victim of battering.[5]

It would be inappropriate and very insensitive to speak as if all abused women shared one experience of suffering, even though violence reveals a blatant disregard for women's individuality. Women of color, immigrants, poor women, disabled women and others do differ in how they respond in the aftermath of violence and in what forms of social support are available to them.

It would also be insensitive and wrong to suggest that all Christian women have similar experiences of healing. While some of the strands in the healing tapestry are similar, each woman's story of help and empowerment in the midst of crisis stands on its own.

For the Christian victim, abuse strikes at the heart of her sense of herself as a daughter of God, created in God's image. Because of this, trust and hope do not simply help in the healing process, they are essential ingredients in healing. Jesus himself struggled between betrayal and hope in the Garden of Gethsemane before his death. He participates in your own struggle and will walk with you into healing and wholeness.

Healing is not the same as "returning to normal."[6] Healing is a process of coming to terms with what has happened as you look toward the promise of tomorrow. Healing does not diminish the reality of the abuse or its consequences. But as you call out for help, God comes into partnership with you.

In the words of one victim: "I know, I couldn't even admit it to myself for years and years . . ."[7] Admitting that you need help is the first rung on the ladder toward healing. Start the climb today.

The journey to healing and wholeness begins with just one step.

FOR SPIRITUAL REFLECTION

Mary and Martha sat in confusion, surrounded by compassionate friends. It was good to have company, but they hardly dared express the grief that almost consumed them. Their beloved brother, Lazarus, was dead—and they both knew full well that it could have been prevented. When his illness had become serious, they had sent for Jesus, confident that their friend would come with his wonderful healing power.

But Jesus simply had not appeared. All through the night they waited and watched and prayed, but the Master did not come. Nor was he there by morning light. And now it was too late. Lazarus breathed his last, and Jesus wasn't even present for the funeral. Their dearest friend had failed them. How could he so betray their friendship?

Jesus had enjoyed their hospitality, even rebuking Martha for being too preoccupied with the kitchen work of a hostess. When she hurried about, anxious to prepare her very best food for him, he had challenged her to think of other priorities (see Luke 10:38-42).

Mary had let go of housewifely tasks in order to learn from Jesus. *She should know better,* Martha had thought. One rabbi had said it was better to give the Torah—the books of the Law, Genesis through Deuteronomy—to be burned than to teach it to a woman. Another said it was better to teach a daughter to be sexually lewd than to teach her the Scriptures. Martha, the older sister, was very aware of proper behavior. Even today in certain branches of Judaism, a woman's salvation is believed to depend on how well she keeps a kosher house and provides kosher food for her family. In all this Martha succeeded and Mary failed.

But Jesus had sided with Mary. It was better, he insisted, for a woman to learn, to be a true disciple. Martha's hostess efforts had left her flustered and unable to pay attention to what Jesus was saying. One simple dish would have been enough for their dinner, and one all-consuming passion should have claimed their hearts.

The story in John 11 makes it clear that Martha had reflected carefully on Jesus' reproof. If Mary had learned from his more general teaching, she had learned from his perspective on the spiritual and intellectual capacities of women. Clearly his priorities were different from those she had been taught.

But where was Jesus when there was a real and urgent crisis? Had he failed to come because others were more important to him than they were? Had he ignored their plea for help because they were women? Did their anxiety and distress even matter to him? Why hadn't he even sent an answer?

But suddenly the word did come that Jesus was approaching their village. The news was only whispered to the sisters, for Jesus' nonarrival had become a subject too difficult to mention among their friends. Mary was too dispirited even to move—better to stay with those who had come promptly to show their sympathy. But Martha rushed to meet him.

Her first words expressed her disappointment and sense of betrayal. "If only you had been here, my brother would not have died!" There it was laid out before him: she was in a faith crisis because Jesus had not done as he had led her to expect. Drawing a deep breath, she ventured, "I know that God will give you whatever you ask."

"Your brother will rise again," he reassured her.

How could he be so callous—first to fail his sick friend and then to talk of the coming resurrection? It was good to remember that the dead will rise in the final day of judgment, but *what about now?* What about their loneliness and grief, the difficulties of two women living alone, the financial hardship, the sense that Jesus couldn't be counted on when he was needed most?

Then Jesus began to stretch her faith still further, presenting himself to her in a new way: "I am the resurrection and the life. Those who believe in me, even though they die, will live, and everyone who lives and believes in me will never die. Do you believe this?" (John 11:25-26).

At the moment of her deepest despair, Jesus challenged her faith. Could she believe that the friend who failed to come is the One sent from God to bring life?

Yes, Lord, I believe that you are the Messiah, the Son of God, the one coming into the world. (John 11:27)

This testimony has rung forth throughout the centuries. So often we admire the confession of Peter (Matthew 16:16) and forget that of Martha in the midst of her anguished crisis. Yet her confession is the linchpin of John's story about Jesus as the Son of God.

Jesus drew forth from Martha a faith that was far deeper than any she could have imagined. In the moment of crisis, our faith either dissolves or evolves. When our whole world falls apart, either we find new meaning in Christ or we brood in meaninglessness. In the Gospel account, both sisters are profoundly changed as a result of the encounter with Jesus that follows Lazarus's death.

Martha was never one to be still for long, and she quickly turned to bring her sister to the Savior and to a new understanding of him. "The Teacher is here and is asking for you," she whispered. Mary's abrupt departure took the other mourners by surprise; they concluded that she must be going back to the tomb.

She came quickly to the place where Jesus was waiting, in the same place where he had met Martha, just outside the village. She fell at his feet and gave vent to her grief. "If only you had been here, my brother would not have died," she cried out.

Then Jesus too began to weep. Far from being callous, he was deeply sensitive to the sisters' loss. Indeed, his delay in arriving, which seemed at first to indicate lack of concern, was part of a divine strategy (see John 11:3-16) even though it could not be humanly fathomed. He had explained to his disciples, "This illness does not lead to death; rather it is for God's glory, so that the son of God may be glorified through it. . . . For your sake I am glad I was not there, so that you may believe." His purpose was not to prevent the death but to call Lazarus back to life, into a life of deeper meaning.

So often women ask, "Where was Christ when I was being abused?" The answer is that he is there weeping, painfully aware of the abuse but allowing humans freedom of will, even to do what is wrong. And ultimately he is there waiting to work justice and to bring healing to the grieving soul.

Jesus asked to be taken to the tomb and to have it opened, despite Martha's most practical observation that her brother's body would already be rotting. It was too late for healing, she thought—a view that Jesus contradicted: "Did I not tell you that if you believed, you would see the glory of God?" (John 11:40).

And then the miraculous happened. Lazarus answered Jesus' call and came forth from the grave. The dead was made alive. The sorrow of bereavement turned to joyful amazement.

Jesus' prayer had been answered: "I have said this for the sake of the crowd standing here, that they may believe that you sent me" (11:42). His purpose was now understood. God had confirmed Martha's confession of Jesus as the Christ who was sent by God into the world.

We do not read of an immediate response from her sister; instead that came during Jesus' next visit to Bethany. Mary, filled with inexpressible joy, poured precious ointment on him and wiped his feet with her hair. Though Jewish women were expected to keep their long hair covered, she had learned how much Jesus values women, and this enabled her to express the depths of her being (John 11:2; 12:3-8; see also Matthew 26:6-13; Mark 14:3-9). John tells of Mary at Jesus' feet, but Matthew and Mark tell of her anointing the head that was soon to be crowned with thorns. Kings and priests and the Christ were to be anointed on the head, and Mary's action expressed her new understanding of who Jesus really was.

As the odor of perfume filled the whole house, Mary was again subjected to criticism, and again Jesus defended her. While others complained that the alabaster jar of perfumed oil might have been sold and the proceeds given to the poor, Jesus accepted her act of devotion and adoration as a personal gift to himself.

We read much of what Jesus did for others but little of gifts or personal kindnesses that were done to him. At his birth, the magi had brought myrrh along with gold and frankincense; and now, just preceding his death, he is again presented with myrrh, the embalming spice. In life his body was shown the respect that would be denied it after his execution as a criminal. "She has done what she could; she has anointed my body beforehand for its burial," Jesus mused (Mark 14:8). In the ancient world, it was the task of women to prepare a corpse for its final rest; but this was not permitted in the case of criminal execution. Joseph of Arimathea and Nicodemus would do their best, but Mary had anticipated them in a beautiful and fitting manner while Jesus still lived.

Mary had come to a place where she could serve Christ in a way that others could not. Of all Jesus' followers, she seems to have been the one who best understood his approaching death. We do not read that she was present at the tomb, for her work was already done. Jesus declared that her deed should be known wherever in the world the gospel was preached (Mark 14:9). Her personal crisis had been transformed into a significant piece of the salvation story.

❦

For twelve years, the woman had been afflicted with a persistent vaginal discharge. According to the laws of Israel, this made her perpetually unclean. Whatever she touched was impure and not to be touched by others. Rules like this had contributed much to sanitation and public health in Israel, but legalistic restrictions had gone far beyond the regulations of the Bible. In essence this woman was an outcast from society. All that she possessed had been spent on visits to one physician after another, and their "cures" had only made her worse. Death was preferable to the constant weakness, the ostracism, the humiliating experience of her affliction (see Luke 8:42-48).

Like others, she had heard of Jesus. But there were always such crowds around him. How could she, the unclean, approach him without jostling others, without calling attention to herself and her wretched condition?

But one day she determined to seek healing. She would brave the crowd, would push her way through the mass of strangers and touch only the fringe of his prayer shawl. She knew of his healing power and decided that just one touch would be enough—after all the years of untouchability.

Among the hordes of people, she was not noticed as she inched her way toward the Master. He had to walk slowly because of the pressure of the crowd, and by crouching low she was able to reach out her trembling hand to the fringe of his garment.

Then, in the midst of all the jostling and noise, Jesus stopped completely. Someone had touched him, he said. But many people had touched him. How could it be avoided in such a mob?

Someone had touched him in a special way, he insisted, for he had felt the healing power go forth. He stood waiting, unwilling to go on until the owner of the hand should be identified, the healing revealed.

Quaking with fright, stammering with embarrassment, the woman emerged and confessed her affliction and the healing she had experienced. Why, oh why, did he demand a public revelation of her most intimate problem?

Jesus seemed not at all offended that he had been touched by a menstruating woman, nor was he disturbed by her underlying gynecological problem. Women's bodies, as well as their souls, were his concern. His affirmation, "Your faith has made you well," placed the emphasis on her spiritual condition rather than on a bodily discharge. Women's bodies were acceptable to Jesus. He concluded, "Daughter, . . . go in peace"— healed, affirmed and empowered.

HEALING FOR ABUSED HUSBANDS

🌹

PASTORS SAY THEY HAVE VERY LIMITED EXPERIENCE working with Christian men who have been abused by their wives or girlfriends. Does this mean there are very few Christian men who have been abused? Or are men who are abused by their partners especially unlikely to seek help from a pastor or from agencies in the secular community? In research studies reported in my book *The Battered Wife: How Christians Confront Family Violence,* 9.7 percent of evangelical pastors had counseled two or more men in the previous year who revealed that they had an abusive wife or partner, while 60.2 percent had *never* been approached for help by a man abused by his wife or partner. By contrast, only 16.8 percent of pastors reported that a woman who had an abusive husband or partner had never sought their pastoral help.

The Bible condemns violence, whether it is perpetrated by a male or by a female. In Proverbs 27:12 we read, "The clever see danger and hide; but the simple go on, and suffer for it." The NIV says it this way: "The prudent see danger and take refuge, but the simple keep going and suffer for it." To be sure, the Bible teaches that one should not put oneself in harm's way.

Men who have been violated should be able to look to their pastor or spiritual leader for help. In our research studies, clergy did report more experience responding to the needs of men who were abused in childhood by a parent—20.9 percent had counseled two or more such men in the previous year. These men have both spiritual and emotional concerns, and referrals need to cover a wide range of sources, much like those we discussed in chapter four.

The pattern of abuse may differ between male victims and women victims. There is very little research published on this subject, but we can gather from other sources that differences are related to issues such as fear of returning home to an abusive partner, economic vulnerability, and extreme power and control rooted in a society still marked by gender discrimination. The context of a man's abuse may be quite different from that of a woman. There is need for more research in this area. But always it is important to take very seriously the pain and anguish of a man who reports abuse.

Appendix 2

GOD'S PATTERN FOR
SAFETY AND PEACE IN HOME LIFE

THE BIBLE'S REPEATED PROMISE IS THAT THERE will be peace and safety in the home of the godly and freedom from terror. Within and outside of their own homes, God's people should be able not only to lie down in safety (Leviticus 26:6; Psalm 3:6; Isaiah 14:30; Hosea 2:18) but also to live in safety (Jeremiah 23:6; 32:37; 33:16; 34:24-28; Ezekiel 28:26; 34:24-28; 38:8, 14).

How very good and pleasant it is
    when kindred live together in unity!
It is like the precious oil on the head,
    running down upon the beard,
on the beard of Aaron,
    running down over the collar of his robes.
It is like the dew of Hermon,
    which falls on the mountains of Zion.
For there the LORD ordained his blessing,
    life forevermore.

PSALM 133

The effect of righteousness will be peace,
    and the result of righteousness, quietness and trust forever.
My people will abide in a peaceful habitation,
    in secure dwellings, and in quiet resting places.

ISAIAH 32:17-18

So Israel lives in safety,
    untroubled is Jacob's abode.

DEUTERONOMY 33:28

You shall know that your tent is safe.

JOB 5:24

You shall lie down, and no one shall make you afraid.

LEVITICUS 26:6

I will settle them in safety.

JEREMIAH 32:37

I will both lie down and sleep in peace;
    for you alone, O LORD, make me lie down in safety.

PSALM 4:8

Thus says the Lord GOD: When I gather the house of Israel from the peoples among whom they are scattered, and manifest my holiness in them in the sight of the nations, then they shall settle on their own soil that I gave to my servant Jacob. They shall live in safety in it, and build houses and plant vineyards. They shall live in safety, when I execute judgments upon all their neighbors who have treated them with contempt. And they shall know that I am the LORD their God.

EZEKIEL 28:25-26

They shall all sit under their own vines and under their
      own fig trees,
            and no one shall make them afraid;
            for the mouth of the LORD of hosts has spoken.

MICAH 4:4

This is what the sovereign LORD says: In that day, when my people Israel
are living in safety, will you not take notice of it?

EZEKIEL 38:14 NIV

They shall live in safety, and no one shall make them afraid.

EZEKIEL 34:28

Their children are established in their presence,
      and their offspring before their eyes.
Their houses are safe from fear.

JOB 21:8-9

Because you have made the LORD your refuge,
      the Most High your dwelling place,
no evil shall befall you,
      no scourge come near your tent. . . .
Those who love me, I will deliver;
      I will protect those who know my name.
When they call to me, I will answer them;
      I will be with them in trouble,
      I will rescue them and honor them.

PSALM 91:9-10, 14-15

All your children shall be taught by the LORD,
      and great shall be the prosperity of your children.
In righteousness you shall be established;

you shall be far from oppression, for you shall not fear;
and from terror, for it shall not come near you.
If anyone stirs up strife,
it is not from me;
whoever stirs up strife with you
shall fall because of you. . . .
No weapon that is fashioned against you shall prosper,
and you shall confute every tongue that rises against you in judgment.
This is the heritage of the servants of the LORD
and their vindication from me, says the LORD.

ISAIAH 54:13-14, 17

A friend loves at all times,
and kinsfolk are born to share adversity.

PROVERBS 17:17

Better is a dinner of vegetables where love is
than a fatted ox and hatred with it.
Those who are hot-tempered stir up strife,
but those who are slow to anger calm contention.

PROVERBS 15:17-18

Do not envy the wicked,
nor desire to be with them;
for their minds devise violence,
and their lips talk of mischief.
By wisdom a house is built,
and by understanding it is established;
by knowledge the rooms are filled
with all precious and pleasant riches.

PROVERBS 24:1-4

Let your gentleness be known to everyone. The Lord is near.

PHILIPPIANS 4:5

Wives, be subject to your husbands as is fitting in the Lord. Husbands, love your wives and do not be harsh with them.

Children, obey your parents in everything, for this is your acceptable duty in the Lord. Fathers, do not provoke your children, or they may lose heart.

COLOSSIANS 3:18-21

Wives, in the same way, accept the authority of your husbands, so that, even if some of them do not obey the word, they may be won over without a word by their wives' conduct, when they see the purity and reverence of your lives. Do not adorn yourselves outwardly by braiding your hair, and by wearing gold ornaments or fine clothing; rather, let your adornment be the inner self with the lasting beauty of a gentle and quiet spirit, which is very precious in God's sight. . . . Husbands, in the same way, show consideration for your wives in your life together, paying honor to the woman as the weaker sex, since they too are also heirs of the gracious gift of life—so that nothing may hinder your prayers.

1 PETER 3:1-4, 7

Husbands, love your wives, just as Christ loved the church and gave himself up for her, in order to make her holy by cleansing her with the washing with water through the word, so as to present the church to himself in splendor, without a spot or wrinkle or anything of the kind— yes, so that she may be holy and without blemish. In this same way, husbands should love their wives as they do their own bodies. He who loves his wife loves himself. For no one ever hates his own body, but he nourishes and tenderly cares for it, just as Christ does for the church, because we are members of his body. "For this reason a man will leave his father and mother and be joined to his wife, and the two will become one flesh." This is a great mystery, and I am applying it to Christ and the church. Each of you, however, should love his wife as himself, and a wife should respect her husband.

EPHESIANS 5:25-33

If the unbelieving partner separates, let it be so; in such a case the brother or sister is not bound. It is to peace that God has called you.

1 CORINTHIANS 7:15

O let the evil of the wicked come to an end,
     but establish the righteous,
you who test the minds and hearts,
     O righteous God.

PSALM 7:9

They shall come and sing aloud on the height of Zion,
     they shall be radiant over the goodness of the LORD,
over the grain, the wine, and the oil,
     and over the young of the flock and the herd;
their life shall become like a watered garden,
     and they shall never languish again.
Then shall the young women rejoice in the dance,
     and the young men and the old shall be merry.
I will turn their mourning into joy,
     I will comfort them, and give them gladness for sorrow.

JEREMIAH 31:12-13

Appendix 3

SOME SUGGESTIONS
FOR WORSHIP THAT HEALS

WORSHIP IS A WONDERFUL AVENUE FOR HEALING. We can contemplate Scripture either individually or within a worshiping community. The words of Scripture can hold us up, even when we cannot form our own prayers.

There are many worship resources that may bring healing to a wounded soul. We offer these as examples of the spiritual riches that victims may use as they are transformed into survivors.

For you, O God, have tested us;
    you have tried us as silver is tried.
You brought us into the net;
    you laid burdens on our backs;
you let people ride over our heads;
    we went through fire and through water;
yet you have brought us out to a spacious place.

PSALM 66:10-12

It is that spacious place that God's people seek, a place of rest that has been promised. For the woman whose life has been in constant turmoil and confusion, these passages may bring healing.

The effect of righteousness will be peace,
and the result of righteousness, quietness and trust forever.
My people will abide in a peaceful habitation,
in secure dwellings, and in quiet resting places.

ISAIAH 32:17-18

The LORD is exalted, he dwells on high;
    he filled Zion with justice and righteousness;
he will be the stability of your times,
    abundance of salvation, wisdom and knowledge;
    the fear of the LORD is Zion's treasure. . . .
Your eyes will see the king in his beauty;
    they will behold a land that stretches far away. . . .
Look on Zion, the city of our appointed festivals!
    Your eyes will see Jerusalem,
    a quiet habitation, an immovable tent,
whose stakes will never be pulled up,
    and none of whose ropes will be broken.
But there the LORD in majesty will be for us
    a place of broad rivers and streams.

ISAIAH 33:5-6, 17, 20-21

Julie Ann Hilton tells of the comfort a group of childhood abuse victims
found in the following passage as they looked forward to God's trans-
forming grace in their lives.

The spirit of the Lord GOD is upon me,
    because the LORD has anointed me;
he has sent me to bring good news to the oppressed,
    to bind up the brokenhearted,
to proclaim liberty to the captives,

and release to the prisoners;
to proclaim the year of the LORD's favor,
　　and the day of vengeance of our God;
　　to comfort all who mourn;
to provide for those who mourn in Zion—
　　to give them a garland instead of ashes,
the oil of gladness instead of mourning,
　　the mantle of praise instead of a faint spirit.
They shall be called oaks of righteousness,
　　the planting of the LORD, to display his glory.

ISAIAH 61:1-4

They were struck with the concept of becoming strong oaks of righteousness rather than wounded victims; they rejoiced in God's planting.[1]

One of the most powerful means of healing is spiritual songs. A
woman can look forward to new wholeness as the Israelites look forward
to the Promised Land and to restoration of God's promises. One woman
found great help in singing a chorus that incorporated the wonderful
promises of Isaiah 62:

The nations shall see your vindication,
　　and all the kings your glory;
and you shall be called by a new name
　　that the mouth of the LORD will give.
You shall be a crown of beauty in the hand of the LORD,
　　and a royal diadem in the hand of your God.
You shall no more be termed Forsaken,
　　and your land shall no more be termed Desolate;
but you shall be called My Delight Is in Her,
　　and your land Married;
for the Lord delights in you,
　　and your land shall be married. (Isaiah 62:2-4)

Here Zion is pictured as a wounded and rejected wife who is transformed and restored, and from this image the victim took the promise of
a new name and a new status as her particular promise. Over and over
that woman nourished her own soul and that of others with her singing
of the song "I Will Change Your Name."

> I will change your name.
> You will no longer be called
> Wounded, Outcast, Lonely or Afraid.
> I will change your name.
> You new name shall be
> Confidence, Joyfulness, Overcoming One,
> Faithfulness, Friend of God,
> One who seeks my face.[2]

Another woman found great comfort in singing the hymn "Light of
the World," which speaks of spiritual sunrise:

> Light of the World, we hail Thee
> Flushing the eastern sky!
> Never shall darkness veil Thee
> Again from human eyes.
> Too long, alas, withholden,
> Now spread from shore to shore;
> Thy light so glad and golden
> Shall set on earth no more.

Each woman may have a song of her own that brings the promise of
healing to her spirit. The heart that is too crushed to read or pray can
still sing the old familiar songs. The singing of spiritual songs is a healing
exercise (see Psalm 33:2-3; Ephesians 5:19; Colossians 3:16). There is to
be a new song for those who await it (see Psalm 30:3; 40:3; 96:1; 144:9;
Isaiah 42:10; Revelation 5:9; 14:2).

LITANY: HOPE IN THE MIDST OF VIOLENCE

Prayer, either corporate or individual, is another avenue of grace. Some may find a litany helpful as a means of raising a united voice of believers. The following was prepared for a special service of the World Evangelical Fellowship's task force on violence against women.

VOICE OF VICTIM:
In another region of the country, I tried to escape from a husband who had attempted to kill me. The women's shelters said they had no room; and although there was a large parsonage with adequate space, the church would not help me even for one night. My family drove a very long way to rescue me; but why were God's people not there for me?

RESPONSE:
There came along the road a priest and a Levite who looked at the wounded person lying beside the road and passed by on the other side.

Is not this the fast that I have chosen,
To loose the bonds of wickedness
To undo the heavy burden
To let the oppressed go free
And that you break every yoke?
Is it not to share your bread with the hungry
And that you bring to your house the poor who are cast out? [Isaiah 58:6-7]

VOICE OF LAW ENFORCMENT OFFICER
The largest category of 911 calls that our Police Department receives are those involving domestic violence. Doesn't the Bible have something to say about what church folk should do when there's a community problem like this?

RESPONSE: Thus says the LORD: Act with justice and right-
                           eousness, and deliver from the hand of the op-
                           pressor anyone who has been robbed. And do
                           no wrong or violence to the alien, the fatherless,
                           and the widow, or shed innocent blood in this
                           place. [Jeremiah 22:3]

VOICE OF WORKER   Women and children need to be protected, but
WITH THE   so do the elderly. In my work, I see a lot of
ELDERLY: abuse and neglect of the senior citizens in this
                           community.

RESPONSE: Pure religion and undefiled before God the Fa-
                           ther is this: to look out for orphans and widows
                           in their affliction and to keep oneself unspotted
                           from the world. [James 1:27]

VOICE OF WOMAN   At a general assembly of the World Evangelical
LEADER: Fellowship, an African woman rose and asked,
                           "When will this organization address violence
                           against women? There are men in this very
                           room who abuse their wives." And that woman
                           got a standing ovation.

RESPONSE: You hear, O LORD, the desire of the afflicted;
                           you encourage them, and listen to their cry, de-
                           fending the fatherless and the oppressed, in or-
                           der that man, who is of the earth, may terrify no
                           more. [Psalm 10:17-18]

VOICE OF WOMAN   In every nation of the world, women have de-
LEADER: clared that their foremost problem is domestic
                           violence. Research reveals that the frequency

and scars of abuse know no faith boundaries. When church leaders and church people fail to hear a Christian woman's call for help, she suffers not only the continued pain of battery but the rejection of her family of faith as well.

RESPONSE: My friends and companions avoid me because of my wounds. My neighbors stay far away. [Psalm 38:11]

Again I looked and saw all the oppression that was taking place under the sun: I saw the tears of the oppressed—and they have no comforter; power was on the side of their oppressors—and they have no comforter. [Ecclesiastes 4:1 NIV]

VOICE OF WOMAN LEADER: In Egypt there is great secrecy about domestic violence. We keep such things hidden.

RESPONSE: For there is nothing covered that will not be revealed, nor hidden that will not be known. Therefore whatever you have spoken in the dark will be heard in the light, and what you have spoken in the ear in inner rooms will be proclaimed on the housetops. [Luke 12:2-3]

VOICE OF WOMAN LEADER: In Australia, a woman evangelist was forced to gather her children and flee the house when her pastor husband grew murderous. Another pastor came to counsel him, but she would not be alive today if she had not stayed hidden that night. How could her life's companion in Christian service treat her this way?

RESPONSE:	It is not enemies who taunt me— I could bear that; it is not adversaries who deal insolently with me— I could hide from them. But it is you, my equal, my companion, my familiar friend with whom I kept pleasant company; We walked in the house of God with the throng. [Psalm 55:12-14] Every night I flood my bed with tears, I drench my couch with my weeping. [Psalm 6:6]
VOICE OF WOMAN LEADER:	In my medical practice in Indonesia, I see unspeakable horrors. Women's bodies are used as trash.
RESPONSE:	If anyone violates the temple of God, God will bring that individual to ruin. For the temple of God is holy, and you are that temple. [1 Corinthians 3:17]
VOICE OF CHURCH WOMAN:	I know from my own experience that God hears the cries of abused women.
RESPONSE:	Your lovers despise you; they seek your life. I hear a cry as of a woman in labor, a groan as of one bearing the first child—the cry of the Daughter of Zion gasping for breath, stretching out her hands and saying, "Alas! I am fainting; my life is given over to murderers." [Jeremiah 4:30-31]

Is there no balm in Gilead? Is there no physician there? Why then has the health of the daughter of my people not been restored? Who then will turn my head into a fountain and my eyes into a spring of tears so that I may weep all day, all night for the wounded of my people? [Jeremiah 8:22]

VOICE OF WOMAN LEADER:

I visit a Christian man serving a life sentence for murdering his wife and children. Like many others, I failed that family. She wrote of financial struggles and the difficulty of finding a church home in which they felt comfortable, never of the other. If it is too late for them, how can we as the people of God reach out to offenders right in our own midst? How can we minister and mentor and monitor, holding them accountable, affirming the person but not the conduct?

RESPONSE:

O you afflicted one, tossed with tempest and not comforted, in righteousness you shall be established, you shall be far from oppression, for you shall not fear; and from terror, for it shall not come near you. No weapon formed against you shall prosper, and every tongue which rises against you in judgment you shall condemn. This is the heritage of the servants of the LORD, and their righteousness is from me, says the LORD. [Isaiah 54:11-17]

NOTES

Pathway to Hope
[1]In 1992 Nancy brought together a research team under the auspices of the Muriel McQueen Fergusson Centre for Family Violence Research at the University of New Brunswick, Canada. Lois Mitchell, Lori Beaman, Terri Atkinson, Sheila McCrea, Amanda Steeves, Christy Hoyt, Lisa Hanson and Michelle Spencer-Arsenault have served on that team. Over the years more than one thousand clergy and laypeople from five different denominations have participated in data collection. Funding for these projects has come from the following sources: the Louisville Institute for the Study of Protestantism and American Culture, the Social Sciences and Humanities Research Council of Canada, the Victim Services Fund of the New Brunswick Department of the Solicitor General, the Lawson Foundation, the Women's Program of the Canadian Secretary of State, the Constant Jacquet Research Award of the Religious Research Association, the Muriel McQueen Fergusson Centre for Family Violence Research, the Fichter Fund of the Association for the Sociology of Religion, and the University of New Brunswick Research Fund. Participating denominations have also provided some financial support as well as in-kind donations of time or resources. Readers interested in a more detailed account of the research methods employed may consult other published work by Nancy Nason-Clark.

Chapter 1: How Do I Know I Need Help?
[1]Based on clergy interview 396.
[2]Based on clergy interview 102.

Chapter 2: How Much of My Story Should I Tell?
[1]*Fire in the Rose Project: Education and Action* (Ottawa: Canadian Council on Justice and Corrections, 1994), p. 3.
[2]Based on clergy interview 272.
[3]Based on clergy interview 106.
[4]Based on clergy interview 106.
[5]Statistics Canada, "The Violence Against Women Survey," *The Daily*, November 18, 1993.
[6]Joni Seager, *The State of Women in the World Atlas,* new ed. (London: Penguin, 1997).
[7]Action, *News from the World Association for Christian Communication,* no. 204 (London: World Association for Christian Communication, March 1998).
[8]"Violence Against Women: Why the Government Has Made Violence Against Women a Priority," UK Cabinet Office Fact Sheet (1998), <www.cabinet-office.gov.uk> (accessed May 2001).
[9]Statistics Canada, *Family Violence in Canada: A Statistical Profile,* Catalogue no. 85-224 (Ottawa: Minister of Industry, 2000), p. 5.
[10]"Facts About Domestic Violence and Sexual Assault," <www.weaveinc.org/facts.html> (accessed May 2001); see also Evan Stark and Anne Fliterart, "Medical Therapy as Repression:

The Case of Battered Women," *Health and Medicine* (summer/fall 1982): 29-32.

[11]Federal Bureau of Investigation, "Uniform Crime Reports: Crime in the United States, 2000," Annual Report (Washington, D.C.: Government Printing Office, 2000).

[12]Murray A. Straus, Richard J. Gelles and Suzanne K. Steinmetz, *Behind Closed Doors: Violence in the American Family* (Garden City, N.Y.: Doubleday, 1980); Murray A. Straus, "Injury and Frequency of Assault and the 'Representative Sample Fallacy' in Measuring Wife Beating and Child Abuse," in *Physical Violence in American Families: Risk Factors and Adaptations to Violence in 8,145 Families,* ed. Murray A. Straus and Richard J. Gelles (New Brunswick, N.J.: Transaction, 1990), pp. 75-91; Scott L. Feld and Murray A. Straus, "Escalation and Desistance of Wife Assault in Marriage," *Criminology* 27 (1989): 141-61; Murray A. Straus and Richard J. Gelles, "Societal Change and Change in Family Violence from 1975 to 1985 As Revealed by Two National Surveys," *Journal of Marriage and the Family* 48 (1986): 465-79.

[13]Donald C. Bross and Richard D. Krugman, *The New Child Protection Team Handbook* (New York: Garland, 1988).

[14]Mary Shawn Copeland, "Reflections," in *Violence Against Women,* ed. Elisabeth Schüssler Fiorenza and Mary Shawn Copeland (London: SCM Press, 1994), pp. 119-22; also see Leslie Timmins, ed., *Listening to the Thunder: Advocates Talk About the Battered Women's Movement* (Vancouver: Women's Research Center, 1995).

Chapter 3: Where Do I Find Spiritual Support?
[1]From clergy interview 342.
[2]From clergy interview 388.
[3]Based on clergy interview 394.

Chapter 4: What Help Can I Find in the Community?
[1]This story was told to Catherine Clark Kroeger; the name of the women has been changed.

Chapter 5: How Do I Get Started on the Healing Journey?
[1]Based on clergy interview 663.
[2]Based on clergy interview 686.
[3]Based on clergy interview 653.
[4]Based on clergy interview 618.
[5]Based on clergy interviews 263, 120, 279, 396, 605, 658.
[6]Based on clergy interviews 279, 272, 388, 663, 394, 396, 376, 663.
[7]Based on a story told to Catherine Clark Kroeger.

Chapter 6: What Steps Do I Take to Get On with My Life?
[1]The name of the facility has been changed to protect confidentiality.
[2]Her name has been changed. In the presence of the social worker responsible for her care, this young woman gave me permission to tell her story.
[3]Evangelical focus group 7, woman 7; story told in Nancy Nason-Clark, *The Battered Wife: How Christians Confront Family Violence* (Louisville, Ky.: Westminster John Knox, 1997), pp. 110-11.
[4]Based on clergy interviews 120, 294, 376, 396, 388, 342, 263, 279; victim's reflections ("Because I took those vows . . .") from Nason-Clark, *Battered Wife,* p. xiv.
[5]For further information, see Nason-Clark, *Battered Wife,* chap. 6.
[6]Three women from focus group 7, quoted in ibid., p. 53.
[7]Jill M. Hudson, *Congregational Trauma: Caring, Coping and Learning* (Bethesda, Md.: Alban

Institute, 1998).

[8]Ibid., p. 12.

[9]Ibid.

[10]Ibid.

[11]Harold Kushner, *When Bad Things Happen to Good People* (New York: Schocken, 1981), p. 3.

[12]S. Rutherford McDill and Linda G. McDill, *Shattered and Broken: Abuse in the Christian Community; Guidelines for Hope and Healing* (Old Tappan, N.J.: Fleming H. Revell, 1991).

[13]Ibid., p. 149.

[14]See Nason-Clark, *Battered Wife*, p. 53.

[15]Marie Fortune, "Forgiveness the Last Step," in *Abuse and Religion: When Praying Isn't Enough,* ed. Anne Horton and Judith Williamson (Lexington, Mass.: Lexington Books, 1988), pp. 215-20.

[16]Ibid., p. 218.

[17]Ibid., p. 220.

[18]This is how the Hebrew version of the story reads, although the Septuagint version (the ancient Greek translation of the Old Testament) reverses the story and has the brothers bring an evil report about Joseph to their father.

Chapter 7: How Can I Understand What Help My Abuser Needs?

[1]Based on clergy interview 277.

[2]Based on research carried out by Nancy Nason-Clark and Nancy Murphy.

[3]Larry Bennett and Oliver Williams, "Controversies and Recent Studies of Batterer Intervention Program Effectiveness," *Violence Against Women Online Resources* (retrieved from <www.vaw.umn.edu> May 2002).

[4]Anne Horton and Judith Williamson, eds., *Abuse and Religion: When Praying Isn't Enough* (Lexington, Mass.: Lexington Books, 1988); Leslie Timmins, ed., *Listening to the Thunder: Advocates Talk about the Battered Women's Movement* (Vancouver: Women's Research Center, 1995).

[5]Edward Gondolf, "A 30-Month Follow-up of Court-Referred Batterers in Four Cities," *International Journal of Offender Therapy and Comparative Criminology* 44, no. 1 (2000): 111-28.

[6]Murray Arnold Straus, Richard J. Gelles and Suzanne K. Steinmetz, *Behind Closed Doors: Violence in the American Family* (Garden City, N.Y.: Doubleday/Anchor, 1980).

[7]James Ptacek, "How Men Who Batter Rationalize Their Behavior," in *Abuse and Religion: When Praying Isn't Enough,* ed. Anne Horton and Judith Williamson (Lexington, Mass.: Lexington Books, 1988), pp. 247-58.

[8]*Word in Life Study Bible* (Nashville: Thomas Nelson, 1993), pp. 1240, 1250.

[9]Many biblical scholars are not convinced by the evidence, but a few have noted the occurrences and their implication.

[10]Katharine Bushnell, *The Vashti-Esther Story,* (Piedmont, Calif.: published privately, 1945), pass., see especially pp. 21-27; e.g., Esther 1:22; 5:4, 14; 7:7.

Chapter 8: How Do I Learn to Trust God Again?

[1]This insight came while I (Nancy) listened to a devotional given by Rev. Cindy Halmarson at the Lutheran Health Care Association Annual Conference, "From Hurting to Healing," January 18-20, 2002, Banff, Alberta, Canada.

[2]For further information, see Nancy Nason-Clark, "Woman Abuse and Faith Communities: Religion, Violence and Provision of Social Welfare," in *Religion and Social Policy,* ed. Paula Nesbitt (Walnut Creek, Calif.: AltaMira, 2001), pp. 128-45.

[3]The material in quotes comes from woman 1, focus group 12; woman 13, focus group 2; woman 2, focus group 5; woman 10, focus group 5; four women talking at once, focus group 16; woman 4, focus group 7; church woman 63; four women talking at once, focus group 16; church woman 43; woman 3, focus group 7. Many of these are quoted in Nancy Nason-Clark, *The Battered Wife: How Christians Confront Family Violence* (Louisville, Ky.: Westminster John Knox, 1997).

[4]Based on clergy interviews 673, 618, 675, 614.

[5]Anne Horton, Melany Wilkins and Wendy Wright, "Women Who Ended Abuse: What Religious Leaders and Religion Did for These Victims," in *Abuse and Religion: When Praying Isn't Enough,* ed. Anne Horton and Judith Williamson (Lexington, Mass.: Lexington Books, 1988), pp. 235-46.

[6]Mary D. Pellauer, "A Theological Perspective on Sexual Assault," in *Sexual Assault and Abuse,* ed. Mary D. Pellauer, Barbara Chester and Jane Boyajian (San Francisco: Harper & Row, 1987), pp. 84-95.

[7]Woman 2, focus group 28, quoted in Nason-Clark, *Battered Wife,* p. 108.

Appendix 3

[1]Julie Ann Hilton, "Isaiah," in *The IVP Women's Bible Commentary,* ed. Catherine Clark Kroeger and Mary J. Evans (Downers Grove, Ill.: InterVarsity Press, 2002), pp. 368-69.

[2]D. J. Butler, copyright 1987 Mercy Publishing. All rights reserved, used by permission, CCLI license 148064.

64124

Refuge from abuse healing and hope for a
261.8327 N263r   64124

Nason-Clark, Nancy
Overton Memorial Library